On Being a Therapist

Jeffrey A. Kottler

On Being a Therapist

Jossey-Bass Publishers
San Francisco • Oxford • 1990

ON BEING A THERAPIST
by Jeffrey A. Kottler

Copyright © 1986 by: Jossey-Bass Inc., Publishers
350 Sansome Street
San Francisco, California 94104
&
Jossey-Bass Limited
Headington Hill Hall
Oxford OX3 0BW

Library of Congress Cataloging-in-Publication Data

Kottler, Jeffrey A.
  On being a therapist.

  (The Jossey-Bass social and behavioral science series)
  Bibliography: p. 155
  Includes index.
  1. Psychotherapists—Psychology. 2. Psychotherapy—
  Practice—Psychological aspects. 3. Psychotherapist
  and patient. I. Title. II. Series.
  RC480.5K68 1986   616.89′14′0924   86-10267
  ISBN 1-55542-213-6 (alk. paper)

Manufactured in the United States of America

The paper in this book meets the guidelines for
permanence and durability of the Committee on
Production Guidelines for Book Longevity of the
Council on Library Resources.

JACKET DESIGN BY JUDY HICKS

FIRST EDITION
    First paperback printing: March 1990

Code 9026

The Jossey-Bass
Social and Behavioral Science Series

In memory of Charles Kottler

🏵🏵🏵🏵🏵

Preface

The process of psychotherapy flows in two directions, obviously influencing the client, but also affecting the personal life of the clinician. This impact can be for better or worse, making the helping professions among the most spiritually fulfilling as well as the most emotionally draining human endeavors. Some of us flourish as a result of this work. We learn from those we try to help and apply what we know and understand to ourselves. And some of us become depleted and despondent. Over time we may become cynical or indifferent or stale.

We have long recognized the impact of various therapeutic ingredients in the changes a client will likely undergo. We know that such factors as modeling, catharsis, empathic responding, intensive questioning, and constructive confrontation will lead to greater self-acceptance and even to personality transformations in a client. But what impact do these processes have on the one facilitating them? Can the clinician be an active instigator of the therapeutic process without, in turn, being affected by its ripple effects? Can the therapist be immune to the influence of prolonged exposure to human despair, conflict, and suffering? Can the professional helper avoid the inevitable growth and self-awareness that comes from studying another life? Can he or she remain the same after being in the presence of so many who are changing? Whether we like it or not, the decision to be a therapist is also a commitment to our own growth.

This process of change and growth works in mysterious ways. I had been working with a client who was exploring the utter predictability of her life. Even with success she felt stale, bored, restless, yet she was fearful of making an abrupt change that could take financial and emotional tolls. I squirmed a little, then a lot. I had just made plans to attend a professional conference I go to every year. I usually have a good time, meet some interesting people, and learn a few things I might try differently in my work. I heard my client elaborate further about her fear of taking risks. I felt even more like a hypocrite, berating her as I had for always taking the safe, predictable route. I did not even hear the last several minutes of the interview so caught up was I in reviewing the meticulous, controlled way I organize my life. Even my vacations. As the session ended I bolted for the phone.

A month later I returned from a snowcamping trip in the wilderness. This expedition, my alternative to a professional conference, gave me time to think about my life, its predictable routines, and several changes I might wish to initiate. My client, too, had changed during the interim—though she had no idea how her crisis precipitated my own. As she related her determination to challenge her habitual patterns I frequently nodded my head. Yet I was nodding as much to myself as to her.

Overview of the Contents

On Being a Therapist is written for all practitioners of therapy—social workers, counselors, psychiatrists, psychologists, psychiatric nurses, and other mental health specialists. It will be of utmost value to students of these professions who may be preparing for a career by learning skills of helping without fully appreciating the personal consequences. Those persons who have experienced therapy as clients, or who are contemplating such a formidable task, will also find the premises contained herein of special interest.

Chapter One begins with a discussion of how primitive healers understand, intuitively, the reciprocal power between participants in the therapy process. A unified framework of the change process is presented as a backdrop for exploring further ideas about modeling and influencing power in Chapter Two. Essentially, all systems of therapy work because they share several nonspecific elements: the powerful "presence" of a therapist/model, active placebos, being with the client, structures for risk taking.

Chapter Three further explores the implications of the role of the therapist as a model by examining the relationship between personal and professional effectiveness. Just as professional skills help therapists to improve their own personal relationships, their real-life experiences are invaluable tools during sessions. This is the best fringe benefit of the field: by being constantly exposed to change there is continued stimulation to promote greater personal growth, which in turn makes us more powerful models.

Chapter Four begins a discussion of the field's special hardships, including the strains of one-way intimacy, fatigue, and personal restraint. Chapter Five covers those occupational hazards that result from contacts with clients who are resistant, abusive, or acting out countertransference issues, while Chapter Six focuses specifically on the emotional difficulties that therapists often encounter. The symptoms, causes, and cures of boredom and burnout are discussed, leading to a further exploration in Chapter Seven of those difficulties that clinicians bring upon themselves. Examples of common self-deceptions are counterbalanced by those attributes and skills a therapist may use to promote self-healing. Additional antidotes are mentioned in Chapter Eight, which encourages the self-application of therapeutic philosophy and skills. Chapter Nine emphasizes greater congruence between the personal and professional in a therapist's life.

Acknowledgments

I gratefully acknowledge the assistance of the many professionals representing the various mental health specialties and theoretical orientations who agreed to be interviewed regarding what it means to be a therapist. While most of these clinicians and therapist educators wish to remain anonymous, their words speak loudly throughout the chapters that follow. I especially thank Gracia Alkema, William Henry, Jerry Corey, Karin Meiselman, and Barry Farber for carefully reviewing the manuscript and providing so many helpful suggestions. Robert Brown, Gary Mueller, James Schmidt, Larry Gusman, Louise George, Lisa Glen, Mary Otto, Diane Blau, and James Danielski also provided constructive input.

I am also grateful for the indulgence of Ellen and Cary Kottler in allowing me the solitude to live this book and then the time to write it down.

Farmington Hills, Michigan   Jeffrey A. Kottler
June 1986

Contents

The Author

Jeffrey A. Kottler is a faculty member of the Center for Humanistic Studies in Detroit and a psychologist in private practice in Farmington Hills, Michigan. He holds a B.A. degree from Oakland University and an M.A. degree from Wayne State University, and he has studied at Harvard University and the University of Stockholm. He received his Ph.D. degree from the University of Virginia.

Kottler has been a Fulbright Scholar and Senior Lecturer at Catholic University in Lima, Peru, and has lectured extensively throughout North and South America. He is the author or co-author of the books *Pragmatic Group Leadership* (1983), *Introduction to Therapeutic Counseling* (1985), and *Ethical and Legal Issues in Counseling and Psychotherapy* (2nd edition, 1985).

On Being a Therapist

ONE ✿✿

Client and Therapist:
How Each Changes the Other

Sitting in a prominent place in my office is a small vial containing an inky mixture of earthen ingredients. It was given to me by a Peruvian witch doctor who believed that clients influence their therapists just as we influence them. He felt that healers, whether in the jungle or the cities, need protection against the evil spirits that emanate from people who are suffering.

According to an ancient Inca legend passed on from one generation of healers to the next, all mental and physical illnesses result from an impure soul. The mental spirit of the healer, his powers of suggestion and white magic, can purify a sick soul and restore inner control. This purification is always undertaken at great risk—for the destructive energy dissipating from a patient also pollutes the spirit of the healer.

Most therapists understand that they jeopardize their own emotional well-being when they intimately encounter the pain of others. Rogers (1972) relates the story of his involvement with a deeply disturbed woman. He vacillated between professional aloofness and the genuine warmth that was to be his trademark. His client became confused, irrational, hostile and even followed him through his relocation from Ohio State to Chicago. As her dissatisfaction with the therapy grew, she became even more critical and demanding of Rogers, piercing his defenses and triggering his own feelings of inadequacy. "I recognized that many of her insights were sounder than mine, and

1

this destroyed my confidence in myself; I somehow gave up *my* self in the relationship" (Rogers, 1972, p. 57). Continuing this destructive relationship eventually led to a psychotic breakdown for the client and to the borderline of a nervous breakdown for her therapist.

I wonder now if Freud's admonishment to remain detached in the therapeutic relationship was less intended to promote the client's transference than to preserve the emotional safety of the clinician. The experience of any practitioner would attest to the emotional as well as the intellectual strains of living constantly with clients' crises, confusion, and intense suffering.

Consider the experience of therapy for both participants. Confidentiality, and therefore privacy, is an implicit part of the encounter as is a level of intimacy between two people that sometimes reaches, if not exceeds, that of parent and child or husband and wife. We are privy to secrets the client is barely willing to share with himself. We know the client at his best and at his worst. And as a function of spending so many intense hours together, the client comes to know us as well. We are partners in a journey.

Influence of Personal Power in Primitive Healing

Central to all that I will say on the interaction between therapist (the generic term for *counselor, social worker, psychologist, psychiatrist, mental health worker, psychiatric nurse*) and client is a relatively unified and simplistic view of change. This framework particularly emphasizes the power and influence of the therapist's personality as a facilitator of growth. The force and spirit of who the therapist is as a human being most dramatically stimulates change. Lock a person, any person, in a room alone with Sigmund Freud, Carl Rogers, Fritz Perls, Albert Ellis, or any other formidable personality, and several hours later he will come out different. It is not what the therapist does that is important—whether she interprets, reflects, confronts, or role plays—but rather who she is. A therapist who is vibrant, inspirational, charismatic; who is sincere, loving, and nurturing; who is wise, confident, and self-disciplined will have a dramatic impact by the sheer force and power of her essence, regardless of her theoretical allegiances.

The first and foremost element of change, then, is the therapist's presence—his excitement, enthusiasm, and the power of his personality. Rollo May (1983) speaks of presence in a different sense—the complete experiencing of the client's being, not of his symptoms or problems, but of his essence. The therapist enters the relationship with clarity, openness, and serenity and comes fully prepared to encounter a soul in torment. The client comes prepared with his own expectations for a mentor, a guru, a doctor, a friend, or a wizard.

One such charismatic healer resides in a village 600 miles north of Lima, Peru, sandwiched between the driest desert on earth and the world's highest tropical mountains at the gateway to the Amazon jungle. This village is noted throughout the world because it has evolved over thousands of years as the capital of therapeutic sorcery. No fewer than one hundred witch doctors actively practice their healing arts here. Chief among them is Don Jose, an old wizard with a weathered, bronzed face and a mouth of broken teeth.

This "primitive" witch doctor, a descendent of Incan medicine men, has an exquisite grasp of the therapeutic principles we use everyday. Although he can neither read nor write and has never traveled beyond his district, he is a master of many sophisticated psychological methodologies to promote inner healing. He capitalizes on the dynamics of cohesion, intimacy, and spectator effects of vicarious learning in his group process. He carefully selects participants for his therapy, weeding out those with a poor prognosis, just as we might turn away those clients we cannot help. He conducts preliminary interviews with each candidate to gather relevant background information and to assess the candidate's mental status. During this time he also plants the seeds for cure by exuding confidence and authority.

Rather than a tweed, vested suit, Don Jose sports a special poncho and sombrero that indicate his status and prestige. His patients travel great distances and pay large sums of money to receive a cure from his hands. Before the ceremony ever begins, his clientele are ready and eager to change. Clearly, Don Jose conveys to them his certainty they will see rapid improvement.

His therapy itself consists of a series of rituals and chants. Processes of catharsis and transference, simple hypnotic inductions, and the use of powerful drugs to promote self-exploration are also used. Underneath all the trappings—the dramatic show of hallucinating and purging on a mountain top—lies a very solid therapeutic regimen that often leads to a cure. Whether evil demons are really being exorcised by the body's spirit or whether an active placebo response is being elicited by a sophisticated set of rituals, there is no doubt that Don Jose and his successful colleagues are powerful human beings. They have presence. They expect their clients to get better. Their clients have faith in their powers to cure.

Therapist Belief and Active Placebos

The therapeutic elements of primitive helping are part of every helping system. The witch doctor, the physician, the therapist, the teacher believe that what they do will make a difference. They have faith in their powers to cure and to promote change.

After a thorough study of all forms of healing—osteopathy, homeopathy, chiropractic, traditional medicine, acupuncture, sorcery, and psychotherapy—Andrew Weil (1983) has concluded that "active placebos" most consistently account for positive results. Even the most intrusive surgical procedures work on many levels other than the obvious. In a then classic study of a miracle cure for angina, surgeons once claimed they could reduce the pain and discomfort of inefficient arterial flow by cracking open the chest and tying off the delinquent blood vessels. Afterwards, the patients experienced a dramatic cure of their suffering. The inescapable conclusion: the doctor's surgical intervention saved the patient.

A study later followed in which patients with the same symptoms were anesthetized and operated on but did not receive the therapeutic procedure of closing off the arteries. Nevertheless, the patients still improved! Weil believes it is the physician's or healer's expectations for a cure, coupled with some active agent (pharmaceutical, physical, psychological), that permits the body and mind to heal itself. In the context of therapy both Frank (1961) and Fish (1973) postulate that most effective systems are designed to maximize the client's expectations for a successful outcome.

The active placebo is set in motion by the dress, setting, manner, and style of the helper and her environment. In our society, diplomas, books, leather chairs, and tweed jackets all feed into the client's expectations concerning a good therapist. And the therapeutic relationship contains within it certain nonspecific factors that influence a client, other than those deliberately intended by the clinician. These placebo effects are impossible to filter out of the process (Patterson, 1985). When the client experiences immediate relief after presenting complaints and initial fears in the first session, both client and therapist begin to feel optimistic.

The specifics of what the therapist does next—whether encouraging catharsis, self-control, or self-confrontation, whether using interventions of interpretation, reflection, or goal setting, whether focusing on thoughts, feelings, or behavior—probably cause less client insight and action than the therapist's belief that they will. The client has faith in us, as people of integrity and wisdom, as experts with the power to heal.

Client Risking in the Change Process

Much of what a therapist does is designed to motivate greater risk taking in clients. When attention is given to the unresolved issues of the past, resistance and apprehensions must often be worked through. To dismantle rigid defenses, to interpret unconscious motives, to reflect on unexplored feelings may involve pushing the client to the brink of her madness. She must confront those parts of herself that have been deeply buried, and she must risk the consequences of relinquishing coping strategies that have worked fairly well until this point. There is a risk, or perhaps even a certainty, that some destabilization will occur. Before real growth can be attained, the client will often experience intense confusion, disorientation, and discomfort. She risks leaving behind an obsolete image of herself, but one that was once comfortable and familiar, and she risks not liking who she has become. She will lose a part of herself that can never be recovered. And all she hopes to gain is the possibility of a better existence. For this she must take the therapist's word.

When the client seeks to modify specific goals and behaviors, the risks are even more evident. To change any single aspect of one's behavior is to set in motion a chain reaction of subsequent aftershocks. One woman had been procrastinating for years in therapy, reluctant to take any action. As is usually the case, all her difficulties were connected—her dead-end job, her desire to move away from her parents, her relationships with men, and her desire to lose weight. If she should make a change in any one of these areas, she would risk everything else tumbling down. To lose even fifteen pounds felt frightening to her since it would mean she would be more attractive, feel more confident, have demonstrated the capacity for self-control, and have proven the power to change. She just could not face the consequences of changing any part of her life, since that would mean every other part would have to change as well. It was much easier to come to therapy each week and please her therapist with good intentions, a cooperative attitude, and a wonderful capacity for generating insights that would not necessarily lead to change.

The therapist's job is to do everything within her power, not just to promote self-understanding, but to encourage risk taking. The client must not only reflect but act. This task is accomplished not only by the quality of one's interventions, designed to reduce the perceived threat and increase the willingness to experiment, but by the genuine commitment the therapist makes to risk taking in her own life. A professional who believes in the value of risk taking is one who has varied experiences in taking calculated chances when the need arises. This courage, as it is modeled in the sessions, begets courage in the clients.

Client and Therapist: How Each Changes the Other

Risks of the Therapist

There are tremendous risks for the therapist in living with the anguish of others, in being so close to others' torments. Sometimes we become desensitized by human emotion and experience an acute overdose of feeling; we turn ourselves off. Other times we overreact to personal incidents as a result of lingering dissonance created during sessions.

I was cross-country skiing in the woods with my wife. The sun was blazing, reflecting off the snow. We were breathing hard, enjoying the scenery and the synchronized movement of our bodies. Quite suddenly, without any warning, I abruptly stopped in my tracks and started crying. Needless to say, my wife was a little surprised.

She asked me what was wrong, especially since a few moments earlier I had been feeling such joy. I finally blurted out the question: "Are you going to leave me?" Again she looked at me as if I were a raving lunatic and replied: "Of course not!" She reassured me with a hug and tried to find out what was going on. I explained that lately in my practice a number of female clients had been working on issues of freedom and independence. They felt trapped in their marriages and resented their husbands' needs for approval and dominance. After years of struggle and resistance from their husbands, they chose divorce as the only solution for liberation. Again and again I heard their words ringing in my ears: "Why is he so oblivious to what I want and what I feel? He thinks things are so great between us just because he finds me home at night. When he finally realizes how serious I am about making changes it will be too late. He has no idea how bad things are and he doesn't want to know."

For weeks the effect of hearing these words in several different keys had been accumulating and had begun eating away at my own illusions of security. Was I, like the husbands of my clients, on the verge of divorce while blissfully denying my problems? While enjoying an afternoon in the woods? Fortunately, my concern was unnecessary, but I felt shell-shocked from the close proximity to other people's battlefields.

Physicians take careful steps to protect themselves from

the infection, disease, and suffering of their patients. Rubber gloves, surgical masks, and probing stainless steel instruments keep germs at arm's length. But sometimes there is a seepage of pain. For one practicing physician (Moss, 1981), all barriers between himself and his patients eroded because he let himself feel too much when his hands were exploring inside their visceral organs.

Throughout the process of therapy, being with the client is our main instrument of cure. Although we try to insulate ourselves, and we successfully pretend most of the time, leaks inevitably occur. As our nonpossessive warmth, caring, and power radiate toward the client stimulating change, so too, do we experience intimacy, dependence, discomfort, transference and countertransference reactions that permanently alter our perceptions and internal structure.

To take on a client, any client, is to make a tremendous commitment to that person that could last years if not a lifetime. For better or worse, no matter how the client behaves, the therapist feels an obligation to be available, understanding, and compassionate. From the moment a client settles himself in the chair for the first time, we take a deep breath knowing that what is about to occur is the beginning of a new relationship. It will have moments of special closeness and times of great hardship. The client will, at times, worship you, scorn you, abuse you, ignore you, play with you, and want to devour you. And through it all, regardless of what is going on in your own life—sickness, births, deaths, joys, disappointments—you must be there for the client, always waiting.

If we ever really considered the possible risks in getting involved with a client, we would not do so for any price. Never mind that we will catch their colds and flus, what about their pessimism, negativity, and psychopathology? You just cannot see somebody week after week, listen to their stories, and dry their tears without being profoundly affected by the experience. There are risks for the therapist he will not recognize until years later. Images stay with us until the grave. Words creep back to haunt us. Those silent screams remain deafening.

Therapist Vulnerability

Watching a therapist enter his office with nothing but a briefcase, one would never imagine that he is preparing to enter into mortal combat. Things appear quite civilized and controlled on the surface, what with the polite greetings and all. But once the action starts, the sparks that begin flying may leave third-degree burns. In a small room there is nowhere to seek shelter. The therapist uses only his naked self (figuratively, of course) as the instrument of treatment, a condition that requires tremendous self-control and exacts considerable vulnerability. To meet the client in a therapeutic encounter we must leave behind our armor and defenses. We must go out from our centeredness as far as we dare. In our effort to be open and receptive, to participate with the client in the relationship, to venture forth as far as we are able, we risk losing our own identity (May, 1983).

Great wracking sobs could be heard through the door, not an unusual occurrence in a psychiatric clinic except that the client had left five minutes earlier. Only the therapist remained —alone, behind the door. Tears streamed down his face. He was huddled in a ball on the floor. The therapist had been conducting a particularly intense session with a man who was mourning the loss of his unborn son. As he was helping the client accept the miscarriage and find hope in the future he realized at some point he was no longer speaking to the client but to himself. His own girlfriend had decided, upon ending their relationship, to unceremoniously abort their baby. The therapist had long ago worked through his loss, the pain, and the disappointment. Yet, it all came tumbling forth again as his client struggled with a similar issue. Against all restraint, all objectivity, all desire to help the client, he lost the separateness between himself and the other.

The therapist is vulnerable not only to the loss of self but to annihilation through assaults on his or her self-esteem. We may profess neutrality without a vested interest in the outcome but we care quite a bit about how things turn out. It is impossible to care deeply for a person without caring about what they do. When a client does not improve or gets worse, we not only feel their pain but take it personally that they are not cooperating with our therapeutic efforts. This is in spite of our attempts to remember the golden words: "We do our part, the client must do his" or "It is ultimately up to the client to change." All of this might very well be true, but we have a lot at stake as well. We can act unconcerned when a client does not improve, shrug our shoulders and go about our business, tell ourselves we are doing all we can, then head for the beach. But others will make decisions about our competence and attack our credibility even if we do not. Family members, for example, having been in the unenviable position of having to live with the client while we only see them an hour or two per week, cannot afford much patience. It is easy for us to tell them: "Give it time. This has taken a long time to develop into a problem and will take a while to resolve." Politely they will thank us as they mutter under their breaths: "This guy doesn't know what he's doing." They will express their opinions to all who will listen, exasperated and exhausted. Since everyone knows a therapist they like, the family's confidence will be further undermined by their friends who suggest they consult Dr. X who really knows what he is doing. And let us not pretend it does not hurt when a client abruptly quits treatment with the following farewell:

"Gee, I know you've tried so hard to help me. And I agree it's probably all my fault. But since I've been seeing you I've only gotten worse. You asked me to be patient and I think I have been, but it doesn't seem to help. My cousin is seeing another therapist, Dr. X. Perhaps you know her? Well, anyway, I'm going to be switching to her. Thanks for all you've done."

Now, not only will Dr. X find out how ineffective we have been (because she is surely not going to assume it was the client's fault), but soon the referral source will call wanting to know how things are going. Clearly, we can make up some excuse about "primitive defenses" or "resistance" that we may even believe, and maybe the referral source will buy it, but deep, deep inside is a quiet little voice that will say: "You blew it." If such an episode occurs in the same week in which we have a few too many cancellations, we are well on our way to a major bout of self-doubt.

Pressure to Perform

Therapy is a performance profession. We are judged by our peers based on our ability to produce results. We must, then, contend with the risks of putting our reputations on the line with every case we take on. We may be forgiven for an occasional lapse, or a client who is particularly stubborn, but we nevertheless feel an assault on our personal as well as our profes sional competence when we believe we have failed a client.

Some practitioners encounter no such self-doubts. Perhaps they are part of a system that allows them to pass the primary responsibility for results along to the client. They believe that it is their job to be there for the client, to listen, and to interpret or reflect when required. But it is up to the client to change when she is good and ready.

Haley (1984) has attempted to change this conception of the therapist's role by placing more emphasis on an active, directive posture. He views the idea of resistance as a figment of the therapist's imagination designed to avoid responsibility for a cure. In strategic approaches such as Haley's there are even more risks at stake—risks for both client and therapist. When the clinician attempts to intervene actively, there is a greater likelihood that the client will be either helped or harmed. The techniques and directives tend to be dramatic and are designed to be intrusive. When they work, they work instantly. When they do not work, some people get very angry. The strategic therapist and other family practitioners thus have even more at stake as far as putting themselves on the line.

The therapist takes many risks with some of her most powerful interventions—those that produce the most dramatic results. Virginia Satir, in working with a conflicted family, will risk tremendous vulnerability and rejection by shaming herself in front of the client. She also tests the trust level in her alliance by disclosing feelings the client may not be ready to hear:

"I want to say something, and Coby, . . . I'm taking a big risk at this moment . . . I feel, and I've been feeling this for about the last ten minutes, that I want to take you in my arms. Not because you're a baby, but because I think in your insides you've had all this longing to have something" (Satir and Baldwin, 1983, p. 92).

Confrontation does indeed take a heavy toll on the therapist as well as on the client. There is no greater feeling of victory for a clinician than the moments after a client responds to confrontation that is well timed and well received. Yet when confrontation falls flat or ignites defensive anger, the clinician may feel thoroughly frustrated. Although the client's safety must be kept firmly in mind, there is no place for meekness and excessively conservative intervention in the therapeutic encounter. We are specifically paid to say things to the client that nobody else has the courage and finesse to say. By giving the client honest feedback regarding his behavior, we risk that he will be unwilling or unable to deal with the reality of his situation. By withholding crucial clinical assessments that the client has a perfect right to hear, we waste his time and money because of our own fears of making a mistake. The therapist is thus saddled with the responsibility of judging just when calculated risks may be taken, when the client can best handle the painful truth. To make an error in judgment could result in a tragedy or at least regressive backlash.

One of the most difficult dilemmas is when we believe a client is a danger to himself and others. Of course, there are guidelines to follow, but they are designed more to protect the therapist from litigation than to help the client. If we have evidence that the client has any serious homicidal or suicidal intent, we are obligated to follow through with commitment proceedings. If we are hesitant and postpone such action to give the client some time to straighten out, we risk tremendous liability if the client should attempt to take his life or that of someone else. And if we protect ourselves and society from the threat of harm, we do so at the expense of the client who will be subjected to numerous indignities.

Therapy is an exercise in risk taking for both participants. If we are not hypocrites, then we are models of change-in-action for our clients. We demonstrate our effectiveness through the force of our personalities and through our willingness to be with the client in a loving and respectful way. We believe in ourselves. We believe in our clients. The elements of change in any theoretical approach converge in the very personal style of every practitioner. To be genuine, to truly accompany a client during his journey of self-exploration requires selfless devotion during forty-five minute intervals. We eventually feel the wear and tear of such devotion, or, alternately, we experience complete detachment from the world and from the feelings behind our professional stance.

TWO ❧❧

Struggles for Power
and Influence

As we are all well aware, growth occurs spontaneously without professional help. Many theories offer explanations of this phenomenon. Psychological growth may be part of our genetically programmed survival instinct or may be reinforced by the environment and society. There are developmental, phenomenological, sociobiological, behavioral, and countless other explanations for spontaneous, unstructured change processes. To complicate matters further, the interpersonal influence that operates in therapy moves in both directions. Just as the therapist attempts to do everything within his power to change clients, so too do clients seek to control the therapist for their own purposes (Strong, 1982). Thus, a two-way interchange of social influence exists between client and therapist, and they have a reciprocal modeling effect on one another (Dorn, 1984). The therapist intentionally and spontaneously mobilizes whatever personal power she has available to intensify modeling processes as these work to influence the client to change. At the same time, the client, reacting to the seductive influences of this personal power, is in turn deliberately and unconsciously fighting for control of the sessions. The client attempts to act out the transference and mold the therapist into someone else. He will also model ways of expressing himself that the therapist will begin to parrot. And as the two people locked together in the combat of interpersonal influence spend enough

14

time together, one of them will begin to reach his desired goals, while both of them will change in ways that neither could ever have anticipated.

Spontaneous Modeling

As the Socratic era of teaching by personal example, Freud's proposal of identification processes, and Bandura's reworking of social learning theory have shown, people are strongly influenced by exposure to other more powerful people. Thus, one main force of childhood is the overpowering urge to grow up and be just like mommy or daddy, sister, Wonder Woman, Superman, teacher, or the kid down the block. Even in adulthood, models in the media continue to exert a powerful influence on people's behavior. Whenever people go to a sporting event or movie, turn on the radio or television set, open a newspaper or magazine, they begin to adopt the values attributed to the image of a celebrity. Caughey (1978) reports on how stars like Johnny Carson or Reggie Jackson invite imaginary relationships in which the public imitates their style of dress, their attitudes, and their behavior. A young and upcoming tennis player admits: "I want to become No. 1 in the world and become a millionaire . . . I want to become like Vitas Gerulaitis, with the cars, the shopping in Paris and the girls" (p. 48).

Even after we learn to stop idolizing our heroes and parents and to prize new values of independence and self-sufficiency, models will continue to exert a powerful influence on the way we dress, speak, feel, and think. In fact, the mentor system is the core of most therapist education: our teachers, advisers, supervisors, authors, and colleagues shape who we are and the way we practice our craft. For many therapists, the first decade of our professional life is spent imitating the master clinicians before we ever consider what we really believe in our hearts.

For most people, unstructured learning is often spontaneously ignited by first exposure to a significant model. Dissonance is immediately experienced when comparisons are made between the model and the self. People feel tremendously inadequate and incompetent after they enter a relationship with someone who appears confident and in control. Yet, there is the birth of hope and resolve. On some level they dream it possible that they, too, can assimilate those qualities they most admire.

Therapists as Professional Models

In the early stages of identification, the model is idealized, made even larger than life. His power is therefore intensified as is his influencing capability. The apprenticeship of the therapist to his mentor, not unlike the relationship between client and therapist, begins in this way and continues through the stages of worship, subservience, dependent love, work, work, more work, mutual respect, and briefly, equality, before the final loss and return to self-direction.

Models give lots of reinforcement to those who express an interest in being just like them. Narcissism pervades our domain. Therapists, teachers, and other professional models such as actors and athletes thrive on gratitude and accolades from fans and disciples. The only difference is that public figures receive financial compensation equal to their aura. Therapists are limited to the ceiling established by their hourly rates. The balance of payment is usually received in the intangible benefits that accrue from hero worship.

In the classroom and in business the mentor or model system has been operating for centuries. In the process of therapy interpersonal influencing power has developed unprecedented effectiveness. Since we are good at managing conflicts, coping with transitions, and heading off predictable crises, the intense trauma associated with "termination" has been substantially reduced. Rarely do clients part company with their therapists seeing them as enemies to be debunked.

Many of the joys as well as the hazards of our field result from the consequences of being professional models. We want to show our clients that it is possible to be happy by the way we live our lives, and this desire serves as a powerful incentive to be fulfilled human beings. Clients know nothing about the details of our existence, our dreams, our disappointments or about what we are like in social situations, yet they know our spirit intimately. They can sense our moods, feel our tranquility, confidence, and energy. They may not know what we are really like, but they know us at our absolute best. We do not impatiently yell at our clients as we might our own children. We try not to meet our own needs at all during sessions. And clients come to love us, to worship our idealized self. Even though we understand the illusions and myths we may be creating, we still have a wonderful opportunity to be more like clients think we actually are—completely loving, giving, peaceful, and in control.

Balance of Omnipotence Versus Humanness

Therapists have become the contemporary equivalent of the oracle perched on a mountaintop; clients are the pilgrims who journey in search of enlightenment (Kopp, 1972). Mistrusting their own inner voice and lacking self-direction, clients look to their gurus for guidance and see them as embodiments of power to worship.

The principal hazard of our profession is the narcissistic belief that we really are special (Herron and Rouslin, 1984). The therapist's office is an unreal world where distractions are minimized and rituals are carefully observed. The therapist controls most of the show. Although the client chooses the content, the therapist directs the script and the interpretation of the lines.

Most therapists do good work. Clients get better. They feel grateful and ascribe their improvement to something or someone outside of themselves. We are more than willing to take partial credit; it is good for new referrals and our sense of potency. The problem is not in feeling that we have made some difference in a client's life, but in forgetting that we are not the paragons we would like to be. When we direct the interacting, questioning, controlling, confronting, nurturing, and even summarizing at appropriate intervals for eight hours a day, it is an abrupt shock to our systems to find ourselves at home or with friends, struggling to be heard like everyone else.

We are used to being listened to. Some people even take notes on what we say, and we can test them later to make sure they were paying attention. After awhile we start believing we are important. Clients and students only reinforce the idea by telling us how much they were helped. Then we remember how fragile the illusion of omnipotence really is. Even if it is initially useful for clients to idealize their therapists, we help them and ourselves to see a separate reality.

Modeling takes the form of presenting not only an ideal to strive for but a real, live person who is flawed, genuine, and sincere. Occasionally, self-disclosure can be used judiciously to close the psychological distance between therapist and client, to increase the perceived similarity. Many clients are greatly relieved to learn their therapist has been the victim of the same self-defeating behaviors they are now trying to overcome. By revealing a model of humanness, with accompanying imperfections, the therapist can help the client feel less overwhelmed and more optimistic that relative personal mastery is indeed within reach. The therapist thus walks a fine line between exuding a certain assurance and personal competence balanced with her unique eccentricities. She must battle with the consequences of acting like an omnipotent guru much of the day and then successfully make the transition to flawed normalcy during the rest of her time.

Mentor's Strength of Character

Most of the great teachers we have ever known or heard of were charismatic individuals. Plato, Socrates, Confucius, Freud, and Marx were geniuses as far as mastering their field's knowledge, but their true talent was in imparting their wisdom and recruiting disciples through the force of their personalities. Contemporary media teachers such as physician Jonathan Miller, physicist Carl Sagan, biologist Lewis Thomas, or sex educator Ruth Westheimer demonstrate the power of attractive personalities in promoting learning. Their followers are as much seduced by their voices, smiles, humor, and presence as they are fascinated by what they say.

The leaders in the field of psychotherapy have made many significant contributions from their research and ideas. However, nobody would have listened to Freud, Jung, Rogers, Frankl, Ellis, Perls, or Adler if they were not captivating people. Their unique ways of expressing themselves, their passion and excitement, their energy and spirit, their commitment and confidence give life to their ideas. It is their eccentric quirks, their personal struggles, their humanity that are so attractive.

Peck (1978, p. 122) tells of his mystical experience in listening to a mentor lecture on a subject that was mostly incomprehensible. He concentrated on the speech with an intensity in which "sweat was literally dripping down my face . . . I was willing to do this . . . because I recognized his greatness and that what he had to say would likely be of great value." Fine (1972, pp. 224–225) also recalls a memorable lecture: "What he said I do not know but I do remember his flashing eyes and the forcefulness of his personality."

Good therapists have a way of communicating similar greatness—that what they have to say is worth listening to no matter how much effort is required to hear. They accomplish this through the intrinsic appeal of their inner voice. The radical psychoanalyst Jacques Lacan was purposely obtuse: " 'If they knew what I was saying,' he offered, 'they would never let me say it' " (Schneiderman, 1983, p. 11). And his behavior was completely outrageous: "Once at Vincennes he told a group of revolutionary students that he could not be expected to have an intelligent dialogue with them because they didn't even know what aphasia was. The students were incensed, and one protested on the spot by taking his clothes off. Lacan responded that he had seen better the night before" (p. 29). Yet these factors only added to his appeal. It was Lacan's eccentricities, his controversies as much as his theories, that attracted so much attention.

All effective therapists intuitively find a way to capitalize on the strengths of their characters. Freud's self-analytic skills, Rogers's genuineness, Ellis's capacity for rational thinking, Perls's playfulness, formed the nucleus for their respective theories. So, too, do clinicians translate their inner selves into a personal style of helping.

The Ideal Therapist Model

With all our differences in values, interests, histories, and training, most therapists share similar attributes as powerful helping models. Many researchers, theoreticians, and practitioners have attempted to describe or even to quantify the dimensions of a therapeutic personality. Rogers mentioned qualities such as genuineness, openness, and acceptance. Carkhuff specified empathic understanding and the ability to respond. Jerome Frank felt confidence was the key to a therapist's persuasive power. Maslow believed the more general striving for self-actualization was a crucial trait.

The ideal therapist is comfortable with herself and appears warm, tolerant, sincere, serene, tranquil, self-assured. This quiet confidence is counterbalanced by a contagious zest for life. Passion. Excitement. Electricity. Enthusiasm. She radiates from body and soul.

We have the client's attention. He is attracted to compassion and a loving nature. Much more than the wooden skills and platitudes of "advanced accurate level empathy," "unconditional positive regard," and other "primary facilitative factors," the therapist genuinely cares about the client's welfare. These feelings go beyond restrained professional respect for someone who trusts us. The client can feel our caring, our intense desire to give of ourselves.

Love is not enough. If it were, parents could heal their children with intention alone. The therapist is a person of wisdom and knowledge. She is an expert in human nature. She is perceptive and sensitive. She is a student of science and the arts, of the abstract and ambiguous, and especially of language. She hears. She sees, smells, touches, and feels with great accuracy.

The therapist is also attractive for her stability and grounding. She is patient, so, so patient. She exhibits great self-discipline, yet, enigmatically, she is also spontaneous and playful. Creativity, humor, flexibility, honesty, and sincerity are other qualities to strive for.

Our main job is to make ourselves as attractive and powerful as possible to lend greater potency to our interventions. We communicate on two levels simultaneously. First, there is the content of what we say—the accuracy of our interpretations, the truth of our confrontations, the appropriateness of our metaphors that make a difference in client awareness, insight, and behavior. On a more subtle, preconscious level, the client also attends to our style. Much of our interpersonal influence, our power as models, operates in the nonverbal realm. It is the way we speak as much as what we say that communicates confidence and favorable expectations. It is the way we carry ourselves that implies genuineness and sincerity in our movements.

We try to teach goodness, honesty, and trustworthiness in our sessions; and such qualities cannot be faked. That is not to say that deceitful therapists are never effective, because some are. But to the degree that we can make our spirit and energy purer, we enable our words to carry even more power. As professional helpers then, our primary task is to be more personally effective and loving human beings. We should show compassion not only in our work but in our lives as well. If we are to be consistent and genuine, then our family, colleagues, friends, and even strangers on the street deserve the best of us as well.

I have always found it ironic that clients who pay for my time, people whom I would rarely choose as friends, nevertheless receive 95 percent of my attention, my focused concentration. Yet, the people I truly love the most get me in diluted form, distracted and self-involved. As I am writing these words my son calls my name. I put him off: "Be with you in a minute. Let me finish what I'm doing." Now I would never do that with a client whose ramblings were interrupting an important thought. I give my best away to people who pay for my time. Must my son make an appointment to get my undivided attention?

How Modeling Works in Therapy

Bandura (1977) and other researchers have described the uses of modeling in specific, behaviorally defined situations. These social learning theorists are fond of investigating those factors that enhance the acquisition of learning, the quality of performance, and the transfer and generalization of behavior (Perry and Furukawa, 1980). For our purposes, however, we are less concerned with the details of vicarious reinforcement processes than with the broader understanding of the different ways modeling operates in therapy.

For example, on the most ambiguous and elusive level, the therapist's energy has a significant impact on the client's mood and conduct. Those therapists who sit peacefully, sagely, speaking in silky and serene tones seem to tranquilize even the most agitated clients. Anxious, high-strung people, those with fears, phobias, and panic disorders, respond well to calm models. They learn from our manner of interaction, the way we sit and stand, the pace of our speaking and listening just how a relaxed person functions. On the other hand, when a therapist's energy is animated, electric, vibrating throughout the room, even the most passive people will wake up a bit. Clients respond to the personal energy we generate. They admire our intense vibrancy and the self-control to modulate it. As models, we remain living examples of constructive human energy.

Clients deliberately and sometimes unconsciously adopt their therapist's speech patterns, favorite expressions, even mannerisms and dress habits. Groups of graduate students can be identified with their advisers from only brief verbalizations as cues. After decades we can still trace remnants in our vocabularies from the influences of significant mentors. With that kind of imitative learning occurring without deliberate encouragement, it is incredible to consider the potential power of strategic therapeutic modeling.

The simplest form of modeling occurs during those instances when the therapist spontaneously demonstrates desirable behaviors. During a typical session, regardless of the content, a client may receive instruction in effective confrontation, appropriate questioning, or comfortably handling silence. Attention may be drawn to the therapist's assertive posture, internally based language, concise statements, or creative thinking.

The use of simulated experiences in therapy provides even more specific imitative learning. Psychodramatic and other rehearsal or role-played structures usually contain a segment that is demonstrated by the therapist. A restrained and timid client who is practicing a confrontation with a family member will be asked during periods of frustration to observe the expert model in action. The therapist will then show a variety of ways to defuse conflict and maintain control.

The same goal of creating greater personal competence through exposure to successful models is also accomplished symbolically. The therapist may tell stories, use anecdotes, or prescribe books or movies as further opportunities to demonstrate effectiveness. The creation of therapeutic metaphors has been developed as an art form to allow clients to experience the vicarious resolution of conflicts without feeling personally threatened (Gordon, 1978).

Metaphoric anecdotes can range from fairy tales to more personal self-disclosures that minimize the psychological distance between therapist and client. By modeling openness, strength, even vulnerability and the sharing of intense feelings, the therapist invites the client to follow the lead. Trust, perceived similarity, and empathic understanding can be vastly improved through restrained, well-timed, and appropriate therapist sharing that is devoid of self-indulgence.

The Uses of Power

Modeling strategies also share a belief in the benevolent and judicious use of power. A clinician's power is first sanctioned by legitimate bodies such as licensing boards. The diplomas on our wall are perceived to endow us with certain mystical powers to read minds. As such, we are perceived not only as legitimate professionals endowed with special privileges but as figures of authority. Depending on the client's previous experiences with other models of authority (school principal, safety patrol, drill sergeant, parents, and teachers), the therapist's power could also instill feelings of resentment and rebellion.

What distinguishes therapists as socially sanctioned models who wield their power cautiously and benevolently is a willingness to subjugate personal needs in the interest of the greatest good for the greatest number. It is the therapist's allegiance to values of personal responsibility, sound moral judgment, and ethical conduct that justify the therapeutic uses of power in modeling (Van Hoose and Kottler, 1985).

If we accept our responsibility as therapist-models and agree to use our influence for the good of our clients, we are then committed to increasing our personal and professional effectiveness. We are involved in the process of integrating our various roles and making ourselves as appealing and as influential as we are capable.

THREE

Personal and
Professional Lives

The practice of psychotherapy permits a unique life-style in which one's personal and professional roles complement each other. There are few other careers in which the boundaries between work and play are so permeable. All the powers of observation, perception, sensitivity, and diagnosis are equally useful with clients, family, or friends. The skills we use in our work, such as empathic listening or flexible problem solving, prove invaluable when helping the people whom we love. In a similar vein, all our personal experiences, our travels, learnings, conversations, readings, or intimate dealings with life's joys and sorrows provide the foundation for everything we do in our therapy sessions.

Fusion of Roles

In their research on practicing therapists, Henry, Sims, and Spray (1973) discovered that most adopt a unidimensional attitude toward all their relationships, whether they be with clients, friends, or family. There is a "distancing aura" in which the clinician detaches himself not only from the therapeutic encounter but from the activities of professional societies and home life. There is also remarkable consistency in the way clients change in sessions and the way therapists made their own decisions to enter the field. Most practitioners were more strongly influenced by personal considerations such as cultural heritage or rejection of parental values than by any professional models. In most therapists there seems to be a burning desire to work through personal conflicts, a conviction to solve problems in others as a way of solving one's own problems, and a tendency to merge the personal and professional dimensions of life into a unified perception of self and world.

The fusion of personal and professional dimensions in a therapist's life affects not only her life-style, emotional stability, and values but the course that sessions take. It is naive to pretend that clients assume complete responsibility for introducing the content and direction of treatment. We may, at first, start with what they believe is their problem, but in no time we have taken over to lead discussions toward the topic we think is most important—whether it be feelings toward parents, underlying thought patterns, or specific behaviors at work. Furthermore, except for the most conservative practitioners who follow the tenets of their theory to the letter, there is a certain amount of inconsistency and unreliability in our helping efforts, depending on what our mood is at the time, what is currently going on in our life, what we have recently finished doing or thinking about, and what we are planning to do next.

It is no extraordinary revelation to admit that events in our lives affect the outcome of our work. But why then do we act as though therapy is simply the application of scientifically tested principles and reliable therapeutic interventions to the specific circumstances of a client's life? We act as though the process is always the same; as though there is always a progression though identical stages, resolution of oedipal and transference conflicts, disputing of the same irrational beliefs; as though the therapist is always a constant. Many of the leading therapists believe that reliability in helping methodologies is the most important issue.

In spite of what we may wish to believe, the practice of therapy is a distinctly human enterprise that is significantly affected by a myriad of random and personal variables. Although it is laudable to work toward greater consistency in the way we treat clients, a therapist is a fallible human being, one who is subject to quirks, biases, errors, misjudgments, and spectacular distortions of reality. Even with the best education, training, supervision, study, and self-analysis, a therapist is hardly the anonymous, perfectly stable, neutral, all-knowing, and accepting creature that clients prefer to see.

Consider, for example, the potential impact of various personal events on professional behavior. Bellack and Faithorn (1981) review several such "intercurrent events" like marriage, divorce, childbirth, moving, illness, and death in a therapist's life and explore how the client's feelings and behavior are affected. Any physical change, such as a leg cast, missing wedding band, weight loss, or the like, can hardly be ignored by the client. Certainly such life transitions and crises cannot be fully shelved by the person experiencing them, even for forty-five minutes while someone else is talking. Perhaps the best evidence of how the therapist's greater vulnerability changes the nature of treatment is the observation that the majority of sexual improprieties occur with therapists who have been recently divorced. It is also inconceivable that a therapist who has a baby growing within her, or pain radiating up his spine, or severe financial difficulties or who has experienced the death of a loved one is going to conduct therapy in exactly the same way as he or she would if these conditions did not exist.

Risking and Intimacy

Intimacy means being open, unguarded, and close to another. To facilitate trust, the therapist must feel comfortable facing intimacy without fear. This closeness helps the client to feel understood and appreciated; it teaches him that true intimacy is indeed possible, that a relationship based on regard and respect is desirable. Through the mutual risking that takes place between the two partners in the relationship, both learn to appreciate better what closeness can bring. Through their willingness to be honest and open, committed to the betterment of the client's life, both participants experience the risk of intimacy.

Keyes (1985) comments on the two most popular messiahs of risk in our culture: Leo Buscaglia and Wayne Dyer. For

very different reasons both advocate risking as the antidote to
boredom. They preach the platitude of our times: "Go for it!"
Each zealously advocates the kind of dramatic risking that creates short-term excitement through hugs or by breaking the
chains of bondage. And both have had a dramatic and mostly
positive influence on their followers. Yet Keyes distinguishes
between these "Level I Risks" common to thrill seekers and the
far more difficult "Level II Risks" that involve the sustained
vulnerability of being committed to a relationship. While the
exciting risk may be more stimulating, the latter variety is far
healthier and more satisfying. Ironically, the two most popular
apostles of risking in the media have both encountered difficulties practicing Level II risking in their own lives.

The levels of intimacy in a therapist's personal and professional life may not coincide. Whereas most of us may be
quite willing to let ourselves be close to our clients, we may not
be so successful at committing ourselves to the intimacy of social
and family relationships. Still, if we stay in the field long
enough, we must eventually confront our reluctance and our
defenses. One therapist admits with candor: "Being a therapist
saved my life. I was about to go into the theatre which is most
unhealthy and rewarded all the phoney, manipulative, narcissistic parts of me. When I chose therapy it demanded of me that I
deal with those issues which I never would have changed in another environment. I made a choice for health."

The decision to work to improve the mental health of others is a choice to improve ourselves in the process. We must confront our own fears of intimacy and risk annihilation of our
identity in every session with a client. We risk not only the sub-
mergence of our self in another but the continual confrontation
with our own vulnerabilities.

Therapist Self-Healing

For the most part, therapists live relatively flexible lives.
Except for those therapists who work in corporate, government,
or other large organizational structures, most therapists in universities, schools, community agencies, and especially private

practice can exercise considerable control over their schedules and work priorities. Supervision and structure are usually minimal. Like the artist and musician, the therapist needs freedom to flourish and create.

The marriage between the personal and the professional in the life of a therapist is never clearer than in the benefits the career provides for its practitioners. Far beyond any monetary, prestige, or freedom needs that are satisfied are the opportunities for growth. "I practice psychotherapy not to rescue others from their craziness, but to preserve what is left of my own sanity: not to cure others, but to heal myself" (Kopp, 1985, p. 12). Just how does this self-healing take place?

We return to the mundane details of what a therapist actually does during the day, not only the dramatic moments of truth when a client finally understands and feels grateful, but the frustrations, repetitions, and stalemates. First of all, therapists have to sit still for long periods of time, and from this we learn physical self-discipline. Rivaling the most accomplished monk, a therapist develops phenomenal powers of focused concentration. We resist the intrusion of external distractions, cars honking, doors slamming, clocks ticking, uncrossed bare legs, phones ringing, unanswered messages winking, and as though in a meditative trance, gently nudge our minds back into the present. With stoic self-control we ignore internal distractions, grumbling stomachs, unfinished conversations, undone errands, the past, and the future and return once again to the task at hand. From such deliberate and studied engrossment, we develop a razor-sharp intellect that is only improved by the things we must learn to remain effective.

Therapists field questions like line drives during batting practice. We leap and duck, catch some and sidestep others. "When will I get better?" "Why do I hurt?" "How do you feel about me?" "What am I here for?" "How do I grow old?" "What should I do?" "What would *you* do?" Whether we respond to these questions aloud or not, we must nevertheless answer them—either then or later. We can run, flee, but there is nowhere to hide. Every working day holds for us a confrontation with the issues we fear the most.

Every time we speak to our clients, we heal ourselves, for there is an audience of two. We talk about what we know or what we think we know, but we teach only what we understand. We feel a tremendous incentive to answer life's most difficult questions and understand things and people. If we analyze the content of our sessions, regardless of clients' presenting symptoms, we will find our most disturbing themes and the things we best understand.

I take inventory of my case load. Tina is learning to stop thinking obsessively, or at least to stop obsessing about her obsessions. She has made progress in that now she only talks about her obsessions during therapy sessions. Whenever I try to get her to talk about something else, her symptoms spill over into her work and marriage. We have learned not to tamper with what is already working, even if it is sometimes boring to listen to. Tina has learned to accept and live with her irritating symptoms. From her I have learned to live with my irritating symptoms, too.

Michelle has taught me a lot about patience. After eighteen months together I finally gave up trying to control or structure our talks. Each week she tells me something is bothering her but she will not say what it is because she does not trust me. I complain that I cannot help her if she will not trust me. She says: "Fine. I'll go find someone else who won't require me to trust him." She keeps feeling better, but I cannot figure out why.

Feeling trapped in her marriage, Rachel used to cry the entire session. But now we play a wonderful game together. Each week she comes in having already decided to take on one of two parts. If she decides to be the dutiful but misunderstood wife, then I attempt to help her feel satisfied with the status quo. She then leaves the office resolved to initiate more open communication with her husband. But the harder she tries, the more frustrated she becomes. (The husband is only interested in work, his model-T Ford, and thrice weekly in the missionary position.) Inevitably, she returns the following week prepared for divorce. We then discuss why she should follow that course of action, but we both know she will change her mind before the week has ended. Twice I attempted to confront her about this circular pattern, but she punished me for my impatience by canceling the next appointment.

These few cases are a profile in diversity familiar to most therapists. Yet there is also similarity in the issues clients confront. And repetition in the things we hear ourselves say again and again.

Taking Our Own Advice

Even the most creative, inventive, and impulsive clinician will teach similar lessons to all her clients. Our moral imperatives, favorite platitudes, and well-worn words of wisdom find their way into every session. Regardless of the client or presenting complaint, there is repetition in the themes we present:

- If you do not take care of yourself, nobody else will.
- Life is a bitch, and then you die.
- We will be dead for a very long time.
- Symptoms are useful in getting your attention.
- Symptoms will not go away until they are no longer needed.
- We are all afraid to be alone.
- If you do not expect anything, you will never be disappointed.
- One hundred years from now nobody will care what you did with your life.
- The material world is seductive.
- Feeling powerless is a state of mind.
- We spend our lives trying to control our hormones.
- No matter what you do or say, half the world will like it and half the world will not.
- You will never have your parents' approval.
- You have less to lose than you think.
- We will never, ever be content for very long.
- It is hard to love without vulnerability.
- Change does not occur without risks.
- We are all afraid of being wrong.
- We do not like the responsibility of being right.
- Everything worth doing is difficult.

If we only took our own advice more seriously. As Penzer (1984) notes: "I have often wondered as I sit in my office at 9:00 P.M. encouraging a father to spend more time with his son why he doesn't ask me what I am doing talking to him at this hour of the night. Nor do I enjoy the dissonance of spending several hours a day playing Uno, Checkers, and War in the name of play therapy and coming home in the evening and casting my children's requests aside in the name of fatigue" (p. 54).

We disregard our own advice, not only by ignoring the messages we repeat, but by failing to implement them in our lives. It hurts to be a hypocrite. Day after day we admonish clients for doing less than they are capable, while an echoing voice nags at our conscience: "What have *you* done lately?" We critically help clients to define those behaviors they would most like to change and end up doing likewise for ourselves. How can we sleep at night if we ask those who came to us for help to do something we cannot do? How can we expect clients to understand ideas we have not fully mastered?

Therapists naturally do many other things that lead to self-healing. Out of necessity we are good at valuing and organizing our time. Because of our training and exposure to the consequences of self-neglect we have an elevated capacity to perceive our own stress. We thus remain sensitized to certain warning signs such as sleep disruption or excuse making or agitation or something in the body and mind feeling out of balance. Once these potential problems are identified we can immediately take steps to correct them.

Therapists work with colleagues who happen to be experts at giving support and nurturance. From the perspective of human contact, we work in an enriched environment. In theory, anyway, our professional relationships should offer the potential for personal fulfillment. There should be opportunities for constructive feedback, for benevolent guidance, and for lots of hugs.

Unfortunately, there is often a discrepancy between what

should be and what actually is. Therapists can be as cruel, manipulative, insensitive, self-involved, and political as the rest of the human race. Fortunately, we are ideally trained to deal with deception, game playing, and politics with minimal threat to the self.

Things We Learn

Perhaps the greatest benefit of practicing therapy is what we learn on a daily basis. Each client brings with him the sum total of his accumulated knowledge, and his primary job is to share the context of his life, complete with all relevant background information. We are thus offered a glimpse into the most intimate world of humanity. We learn about the customs, language, and culture of diverse ethnic groups. We are exposed to differences in Italian, Caldean, Indian, Jewish, black, or Native American family structures. We learn about religions, unique foods, and even the most intimate details of sexual and social behavior.

As we immerse ourselves in our clients' lives, we naturally spend much time learning what people do for work. We learn not only about conventional careers but also about those on the fringe of society. In any given week we may learn about life as a professional athlete, politician, engineer, prostitute, or factory worker. As a by-product of our therapeutic digging, we find out the most interesting details of how corporate decisions are made, how drug deals are consummated, how a poem is created, how clothing is most easily stolen, what waiters secretly do to customers they do not like, how the stock market works, how a tennis player trains, how someone is really elected to office, how an assembly worker copes with boredom on the line, how a seventh grader tries to win friends and influence people, how an advertising writer thinks up ideas, how a policeman controls his aggressive urges, or how another therapist deals with burnout.

One particularly fascinating area of human activity that is accessible to us is what people do when they are alone. I do not mean the usual nose picking or masturbating, but the diverse range of behaviors and activities that occupy people's time when nobody else is around. We learn about people who lack self-esteem and solid defenses, who are so afraid of being alone they will do almost anything for distractions. We meet the exercise fanatics, the ultramarathoners who run for two to three hours a day. Some people use books as an escape; for others, drugs work even better.

We have the privilege of knowing what people really think, feel, and do when their guards are down. And we get paid for it. Not only does the information we gain from clients help us to better understand them; such knowledge also helps us to better understand ourselves. Steinzor (1972, p. 183) comments: "Such vicarious pleasures do much to help me accommodate to lives I can never live. Yet these unsolicited, unintended gifts also provide the context for the continuous rearousal and reinterpretation of my own anguish."

The work of the therapist can be so interesting and so personally relevant as well as professionally satisfying that I sometimes (but not for very long) feel the urge to pay my clients for what they teach me. Yet it takes incredible energy to do good therapy for very long. Thus I both resent and feel grateful for the incentive to constantly challenge myself.

Not only do therapists learn from their clients, but therapists' personal curiosity often complements their professional inquiry. The training programs of therapists, whether in medicine, education, psychology, or social work, emphasize an interdisciplinary perspective to integrate the study of mind and body. Biochemistry is a prerequisite for understanding the organic basis of many emotional disorders as well as the actions of psychopharmacological medication. Neurophysiology is necessary for the differential diagnosis of psychosomatic illnesses. Sociology, social psychology, sociobiology, and social anthropology help explain the social context of symptoms. Educational psychology provides theories of learning and development that we use for facilitating healthy growth. Philosophy and general systems theory help the therapist to reason logically, to organize knowledge, and to formulate coherent explanations for physical and spiritual phenomena.

Freud found the fiction of Dostoyevsky, Sophocles, and Shakespeare, the sculpture of Michelangelo and Leonardo, the philosophy of Mill and Nietzsche to be the inspiration for his theories. It was not his formal medical training as much as his readings of *King Lear, Hamlet, Oedipus Rex,* and *The Brothers Karamazov* that formed the cornerstone of his theories. Freud was first and foremost an integrationist who was able to draw on the wisdom of poets, sculptors, neurologists, philosophers, playwrights, and his patients to create a unified vision of the human world.

In the tradition of Freud, many of his disciples educated themselves as generalists with influences from diverse academic disciplines. Jung, for example, was heavily influenced by his Latin and theological studies as well as by the philosophy of Goethe, Schopenhauer, and Kant, and the practitioners of the new service of psychiatry. Rollo May, the North American champion of existentialism, described perhaps the most pragmatic recipe for a style of therapy that used ingredients from philosophy (Kierkegaard, Nietzsche, Heidegger), psychoanalysis (Freud), phenomenology (Merleau-Ponty, Husserl), art (Cézanne, Van Gogh), theology (Marcel, Jaspers), literature (Sartre, Camus, Kafka), and the concentration camps (Frankl). There is, therefore, great historical precedent in our field for learning as much as we can about everything. Ours is a science of experience, not only from formal research and case conferences, but from literature, that aids our understanding of the complexities of emotion and behavior. Without Shakespeare's plays, Dostoyevsky's novels, or James's short stories, our knowledge of anguish and conflict would be hollow, our self-revelations would be one-dimensional.

Uses and Abuses of Self-Disclosure

Personal and professional issues most clearly intersect in the decision concerning how much to disclose during sessions. If the therapist is reserved and aloof, she risks alienating the client and creating interactions that could become wooden and stale. If she is too open and self-revealing, she risks diminishing the client's importance.

The value of self-disclosure is reported by Polster (1972) in his experiences as a client with Fritz Perls. At first, like most people, he was enamored with Perls's flamboyance but noticed Perls could be very tough and cutting. He found Perls intimidating and unapproachable, and so he remained passive, withdrawn, and silent during group sessions. During a break, Perls took him aside and related the story of his own fear of speaking in public, which had plagued him until a few years previous. For Polster, this was a breakthrough: "I was amazed and felt the gift he was giving me" (p. 154). In later sessions, he was able to share knowing that even (and especially) the leader could empathize.

By revealing part of herself, the therapist indicates her emotional involvement in the sessions. Professional detachment is set aside, sometimes for the benefit of the client, at other times to meet some personal need on the part of the clinician. This sharing can be among the most powerful tools to encourage further sharing by the client (Jourard, 1971). When used in a timely and restrained manner, such self-disclosure can build a more authentic (Bugental), congruent (Rogers), transparent (Jourard), genuine (Carkhuff), and open (Kaiser) relationship (Curtis, 1982).

Kopp (1972) describes the illustrious history of masters instructing their pilgrims primarily by disclosing themselves. The mystics, monks, masters, the ancient philosophers, healers, and teachers all promoted growth through their personal parables. "When I work with a patient, not only will I be hearing his tale, but I shall be telling him mine as well. If we are to get anywhere, we must come to know one another. One of the luxuries of being a psychotherapist is that it helps to keep you honest. It's a bit like remaining in treatment all of your life. It helps me to remain committed to telling and retelling my tale for the remainder of that pilgrimage that is my life" (p. 17).

Yet there are few therapeutic activities that are so abused under the guise of being helpful. Excessive self-disclosure may be done to relieve the therapist's own discomfort with the inherent inequality of the relationship (Herron and Rouslin, 1984). Afterwards, it is easy to find some clinical justification: "I'm only trying to make the client feel comfortable" or "I thought he might feel less alone in his pain" or "I am only being real." If self-disclosure is not moderated, all the barriers between the personal and the professional become muddled, and the client's fundamental perceptions of therapist competence and empathy may be irrevocably altered (Curtis, 1982). Transference is also sacrificed when the therapist relinquishes his nonpersonhood in favor of an authentic relationship.

Yet, Yalom (1980) believes that personal concealment for the sake of transference only denies the client the opportunity to experience a more genuine, loving encounter. These sentiments are also echoed by Anna Freud (1954): "I feel that we should leave room somewhere for the realization that analyst and patient are also two real people of equal adult status, in a real relationship to each other."

Whether at the lecture podium, in the media, when writing, teaching, or counseling, self-disclosure is most effective when the therapist adheres to a personally developed set of standards that best bring out her personality with professional restraint. We wish to communicate our warmth, authenticity, and distinct humanness without diminishing our authority, expertise, and power. Such a balance can be reached if the practitioner asks herself a few questions:

- What do I hope this will accomplish?
- Is there another way of making the same point?
- What do I risk by not sharing myself?
- To what extent am I attempting to meet my own needs?
- Is this the right time?
- How can I say this most concisely?

- How will the client personalize what I share about myself?
- How can I put the focus back on the client?

Certainly there is little time to consider these self-queries in the instant before we speak. Nevertheless, such a vigilant attitude should be developed in order to avoid the narcissistic lapses possible for those crossing the professional-personal barrier. Whenever we give away any part of ourselves, clients feel grateful, although they may sometimes stop to consider why. We can be most helpful by presenting to them only those parts of ourselves that help them to see themselves more clearly.

Personal Fallout

Combs, Avila, and Purkey (1971) discuss the confusion of personal and professional selves in that we can apply a philosophy of psychological mindedness in our private life, but we can hardly practice counseling without complicating personal relationships: "The self is what one is and so must be the same in all of life's situations" (p. 295).

We keep a vigilant eye on personal fallout to protect our family and friends from the intensity of our professional life. Yet with all the restraint we must exercise in order to follow the rules regulating our conduct during working hours, it is difficult to not be abusive, surly, or self-indulgent with our loved ones. All day long we have stifled ourselves, censored our thoughts and statements, and disciplined ourselves to be controlled and intelligent. And then we make an abrupt transition to go home. Much of the pressure that has been building all day long as clients have come in and dumped their troubles finally releases as we walk through the door. If we are not careful, our families will suffer the emotional fallout.

The final interchange between the personal and professional in the life of a therapist has its impact in the amount of time we spend in self-reflection. After all the training we received in psycho-diagnostics, recognizing defense mechanisms, perceiving things as they are, diffusing game playing, we are creatures exquisitely designed to smell self-deception and set things right—not just when the meter is running during therapy, but instinctively when we are alone. Even if we do not deliberately keep track of how our work is currently affecting our emotional health, or how our personal life is affecting our therapy, such an evaluation will take place effortlessly. We find ourselves feeling self-conscious in a social situation, feel our hearts beating quickly, and immediately start talking to ourselves the way we would to a client. Or we make an interpretation during a session that is obviously off the mark and then begin to question what inside us led our clinical judgment astray.

The content of our therapeutic metaphors comes from our personal experience. Much of what we say to clients is strongly influenced by what we have read and seen, who we have encountered, and what we have done that very week. I read a bedtime story to my son and the image of *The Giving Tree* (Silverstein, 1964) follows me into talks with a narcissistic client. Another person complains in anguish of feeling trapped, and I find myself describing a moving passage from *Ironweed* (Kennedy, 1983). I plant trees over the weekend and weave together for a disoriented young man an example of how each living thing requires nourishment, minimal shocks to the system during transplanting, and individual attention. The places I visit, the weather, dreams, memories, everything that filters through my senses all affect what I do during sessions. My work in any given moment is the product of who I have become up to that very instant. As I change so does the style of my therapy.

We, like our clients, change only at a pace that we are comfortable with. If we move too quickly, with a client or with ourselves, the personal fallout reaches dangerous levels. Yet it takes such incredible energy and commitment not to lose ground, much less change one's position. We move just as fast as we can:

> "Now! Now!" cried the Queen. "Faster! Faster!" And they went so fast that at last they seemed to skim through the air, hardly touching the ground with their feet, till suddenly, just as Alice was getting quite exhausted, they stopped,

and she found herself sitting on the ground, breath-
less and giddy."

The Queen propped her up against a tree,
and said kindly, "You may rest a little now."

Alice looked round her in great surprise.
"Why, I do believe we've been under this tree the
whole time! Everything's just as it was!"

"Of course it is," said the Queen. "What
would you have it?"

"Well, in *our* country," said Alice, still pant-
ing a little, "you'd generally get to somewhere
else—if you ran very fast for a long time as we've
been doing."

"A slow sort of country!" said the Queen.
"Now HERE, you see, it takes all the running you
can do, to keep in the same place. If you want to
get somewhere else, you must run at least twice as
fast as that!" [Carroll, [1873] 1981, p. 127].

We all run just as fast as we can, although we sometimes
seem to stay in the same place, reworking the same issues again
and again. In a typical psychiatric clinic, a dozen colleagues
were asked how their values, old baggage, and new dreams influence their style of helping. One psychologist lost her mother
to cancer while still a child and somehow finds a way to diag-
nose all psychopathology as a form of mother-child deprivation.
She views her primary role as providing the maternal nurturance
that she herself so longs for. A social worker has had great difficulty dealing with authority and anger. Not coincidently he
specializes in work with adolescents who inappropriately act
out their hostility. Another psychologist has struggled since
childhood with obsessive thinking and her fear of going crazy.
In her practice she requests the most disturbed referrals and
prefers working with psychotics. A family counselor prizes
humor and spontaneity above all other human experiences and
so functions as a court jester to make people laugh. Such a cor-
relation between the major themes of our personal lives and
our professional style of practice is something most of us can

identify with. In spite of our best efforts to separate the two roles, the barrier remains permeable.

The Human Dimension of Being a Therapist

I recognize the compatibility between the personal and professional in my own life for a number of reasons. First and foremost because it makes my work more fun. I find greater meaning in everything I do when I can relate it to the rest of my life. I like the feeling that I am always working, always thinking, and always trying to make sense of what is happening, and yet I am never working since even time spent with clients helps me to learn more about the world and myself. Secondly, I monitor the interaction between my personal and professional lives to protect both my clients and my family. I know I have unresolved personal issues that get in the way of my being more effective with my clients. I must constantly guard against my self-indulgences, egocentricity, and narcissism. I frequently catch myself saying and doing things in sessions for my own entertainment. I ask questions only to satisfy my curiosity. I let clients dig themselves in holes just to see how they will get out. I inflate my sense of importance so clients will admire me more. I probably see clients longer than is absolutely necessary because I need the money. Oh, I justify all of these actions, convincing myself they are all for the client's good. I do not worry as much about this personal fallout because I am aware of it. I do genuinely worry about those instances when I do not catch myself meeting my own needs.

In all of these factors that connect the personal with the professional, the therapist is seen as a complex being with conflicting desires and multiple urges motivated by altruism, egocentricity, and self-interest. It is difficult, if not impossible, to filter personal elements out of a therapist's professional work, or to restrict clinical perceptions and skills to the office. Henry, Sims, and Spray (1973) and other researchers only confirm what most practitioners know intuitively: that our therapeutic perspective on life is our greatest asset and greatest liability. Being a therapist affords us the opportunity for continual spiritual, intellectual, and emotional growth. We become more intuitive, better risk-takers and communicators. We experience excitement, human intensity, confidence, and self-fulfillment. All at great expense. The consuming nature of therapeutic work only reminds us of a universal truth we so often repeat to clients: every joy has its price, whether we pay now or on the installment plan.

FOUR 🙣🙣

Hardships of
Therapeutic Practice

The marriage between the personal and the professional in the life of a therapist not only provides an enriched form of work but some special hardships. The clinician's life is fraught with draining days, intense pressures, and personal risks. Those who become too involved in their work pay a dear price in giving up leisure time and a private life; those who too assertively distance themselves from therapeutic sessions risk emotional sterility in other relationships.

Ours is a life of mobility. The turnover and burnout rates of therapists functioning in organized mental health settings are frightening. Those in private practice switch clinic affiliations as they would cars. Temptations of more money or power, a roomier office, or more freedom lure practitioners in a game of musical chairs. And, if you stay too long in one place, colleagues begin to wonder why you do not leave.

The various specialties within therapy present their special stresses and problems. In addition to the hazards associated with seeing clients and functioning within an organization, each practitioner must confront identity problems he inherited with his training. As we all know, status, power, competence, and expertise are not divided equally among the specialties practicing therapy. Psychiatrists, for example, must contend with their lack of early training in therapy and an orientation toward the medical model that brands them among fellow physicians as quacks who do not do anything and among their nonmedical colleagues as pill-doctors who try to do too much.

Many social workers struggle with the obsolete public image of their profession as do-gooders who chat with people in their homes. Within the mental health network they fight for parity with psychologists who have their own problems trying to prove what they can do best. Psychiatric nurses and mental health counselors quietly go about their therapeutic work, but they are often frustrated by their lack of recognition. Each clinician, regardless of her chosen specialty and work setting, carries a tremendous burden into a therapy session before the client even opens his mouth.

Occupational Hazards

It was Freud ([1937] 1950) who first suggested that therapists submit themselves for further treatment every five years because of the regressive effects caused by constant contact with clients' emotionally charged issues. Freud moved his clients to the couch only because he could not stand looking at them all the time. That such a reclining position facilitated free association was incidental.

In the face of incredible emotional arousal—anger, sadness, panic, despondency, conflict—the therapist is expected to maintain neutrality, detachment, frustration tolerance, empathy, alertness, interest, and impulse control without feeling depleted, deprived, and isolated (Bellack and Faithorn, 1981). As if such demands are not enough, we are also supposed to be charming and invigorated by the time we get home. Since our friends and family know what we do for a living, they have greater expectations that we will be inhumanly patient, forgiving, and compromising during those instances when they have us locked in battle.

One social worker has worked for the state department of social services for twelve years. She is completely entrenched in the system—politically, emotionally, and financially. She is also cynical, aloof, and sarcastic. Her job description as senior clinician sounds as though it were written by a naive, altruistic academic. There is little time to spend with her clients since most of her energy is devoted to keeping her position in the ever-changing power hierarchy. She is afraid of the abused women she must treat—they seem so pathetic and remind her too much of the way she feels. She commutes forty-five minutes into the city each day, replaces the hubcaps on her car as they vanish into that place wherever hubcaps go, and is patiently waiting for eighteen more years to pass so she can retire. She feels old at thirty-four. She has seen too much of man's inhumanity to man. She has nightmares about broken people without hope; she sees the faces of children dotted with cigarette burns. She cannot leave the system since she has a vested interest in the retirement plan. Besides, where would she go?

A psychologist teaches at the university and consults with local mental health agencies. His professional life is varied as he routinely switches roles from researcher to teacher to clinician to administrator. He did not perish in the struggle to publish. He is well-respected by his colleagues, feared by his students, and admired by his clients who understand little of what he says. He has carefully nurtured his reputation in the community. As time moves on, his lecture notes become frayed, their folders yellow. Each year he gets older, but he continues to meet the stoney faces of students who are always nineteen. If they have talked to friends who had him last semester, they have already heard his best jokes and learned the answers to the final exam. He has taught the educational psychology class thirty-seven times. Thirty-seven times he has heard himself say, "Welcome to Ed Psych. There will be two examinations . . ." wondering what this has to do with learning about helping people. Students rarely come to visit so he spends much of his time in the university senate or on departmental, curriculum excellence, and promotional review committees. For fun he waits for his sabbatical once every seven years so he can catch up on all the computer data that have been piling up on his bookshelves.

A psychiatrist in private practice appears to have the best of all worlds—a lucrative and successful case load, freedom, self-employment, self-direction, status, and power. Yet, he is trapped by his own ambition and greed. He conducts fifty-five sessions per week, neglecting his health, family, and leisure pursuits in order to gross $250,000 per year. What is there to envy? His accountant puts him in limited partnership real estate ventures to shelter his income. As long as he maintains his productivity he will make out like a bandit on his tax returns. But if his income falls, he will have wasted all his energy. His capital is tied up in investments. His cash flow is dependent on his earnings. The tax shelters are useless unless he can sustain or increase his income. He cannot take a vacation without feeling guilty. He grudgingly decides to spend a week in Bermuda but occupies himself figuring out that the hours he is spending lying on the beach are costing him $300 in lost income—plus his expenses. He cannot wait to get back to his office.

The preceding examples of how a few professionals experience the hardships of therapy are not meant to portray the majority of therapists, and certainly very few of those readers who would ever purchase and read a book on the personal consequences of practicing therapy. Nevertheless, we all know practitioners who have let the side effects of therapeutic work really get to them. We shudder at the thought that it could be happening to us at this very moment. And what is the "it" that infects the nervous system of people who try to help others for a living? How do our clients get to us, unravel our precious control, haunt us with their fears?

Sleepless Nights

Clients bring us their nightmares, drop them in our lap, and then leave us to sort them out for ourselves. They have been enduring sleepless nights for years. Now the challenge for us is to keep away their demons. Especially at night, when we are relaxed, and our defenses are down, images creep into our dreams, or if we are lying awake, they invade our peace. We toss and turn, probably in synchrony with the very client who infected us.

The novelist Jim Harrison (1984, p. 17) describes a night I remember poignantly but prefer not to repeat:

Insomnia opens the door to previously un-
traced memories, makes a mockery of the good
sense that possesses us at high noon, and any effort
we make to channel our thoughts twists the energy,
rebukes us with half-finished faces, sexless bodies;
we learn again that our minds are full of snares,
knots, goblins, the backward march of the dead,
the bridges that end halfway and still hang in the
air, those who failed to love us, those who irrep-
arably harmed us, intentionally or not, even those
we hurt badly and live on incapsulated in our re-
gret. The past thrives on a sleepless night, reduces
it to the awesome, distorted essence of all we have
met.

Any client's story could be the trigger, but there is usually one particularly sad or terrifying tale that returns to haunt
us when we are alone in the dark. We tell ourselves it was someone else's misery, but by then it is too late: the chain reaction
has started, and we are probing deeply into our own failures.

One image brought to me by a client will haunt me until
I die. Even though I had read stories and seen movies about this
sort of thing, I could never have been prepared for the intensity
I would feel being so close to someone who had been really ter-
rorized. One day, when she was living in a faraway city, she
ran into an old high school friend who was on vacation. Although more of an acquaintance than a good friend, she nevertheless knew him quite well since he had been her senior class
president. They were delighted to run into each other after so
much time and in such a large city. They stopped to have coffee, to chat, and to catch up on their lives. Then, they parted
ways. She went back to her apartment and, as was her habit,
read stories to her little girl until she fell asleep and then began
studying at her desk. Several hours later there was a knock at
the door. She asked who it was and heard her high school
friend's voice say that he had brought something she forgot. As
her hand hovered over the handle she saw her daughter standing

in her bedroom doorway. She was momentarily distracted as she swung open the door and turned to see her friend with a disfigured, hideous grin and a butcher knife raised in each hand. Although she eventually recovered from her wounds, she would never again open a door without taking some evasive action. And she has never since had a peaceful night.

It has been a year since I heard this story. I still hesitate before I open doors to strangers. And late at night, I see the hideous faces from my past coming at me with big knives.

One-Way Intimacy

Kovacs (1976) considered the tragic flaw of most therapists to be not the need for intimacy but its avoidance. Only within the sterile, ritualized context of a therapeutic session where the clinician is a boss and observer can he feel safe. There the therapist can experience loving relationships but can avoid the risks associated with real family conflict. May (1985) speculates that one reason why people become therapists is because they were used to assuming that role in their families. Henry, Sims, and Spray (1973) discovered in their study of therapists that the great majority of their families were conflict ridden, and Burton (1972) found in his sample of famous clinicians that most experienced great pain or illness in childhood. Whether we actually got started in the helping profession to save the world, to save our families, or to save ourselves, we enjoy getting close to others and helping to solve their problems. Yet, the intimacy a therapist experiences with clients is strange. There are rules and structures, even payment for attention. The therapist must become involved but must not lose his objectivity. He must be intensely concerned but must stay neutral. He must give of himself completely but must not expect or solicit anything outside of a fee in return. He must get close but must not touch.

Apparently, in spite of the prohibitions, rules, laws, we have quite a difficult time maintaining one-way intimacy in client relationships. Taken to its extreme, some clinicians even promote sexual contact with clients under some obscure therapeutic rationale. Shepard (1972), for example, encouraged an orgy during group therapy and afterwards gave what he imagined was constructive feedback to his clients: "I'm sorry that it all happened. I feel lousy. This was the first time in years that I got sexually involved when I didn't want to be. Jane, you have an odor that might drive some men to ecstacy, but it turned me off in spite of my liking you. My best moments were spent alone" (p. 87).

Malpractice suits against therapists for sexual misconduct are skyrocketing. In spite of the haughty indignity from a number of professionals who justifiably condemn such client abuse, it is so easy to see how it could happen, especially since 87 percent of practicing therapists admit to feeling sexually attracted to their clients (Pope, Keith-Spiegel, and Tabachnick (1986). In Fitzgerald's *Tender Is the Night* (1933, p. 174), the patient confronts her therapist:

> "You like me?"
> "Of course."
> "Would you—" They were strolling along toward the dim end of the horseshoe, two hundred yards ahead. "If I hadn't been sick would you—I mean, would I have been the sort of girl you might have—oh, slush, you know what I mean."
>
> He was in for it now, possessed by a vast irrationality. She was so near that he felt his breathing change but again his training came to his aid in a boy's laugh and a trite remark.

Dr. Diver loses the struggle to keep his distance. The boundaries crumble in a searing kiss. They marry. Divorce. He vanishes into obscurity. Tender is the night, but, oh, so cruel is the blinding light of day. And we are reminded once again of the fragile front we try so hard to maintain. To love someone unconditionally, nonpossessively, nonsexually, with warmth, empathy, and genuineness is exhausting.

We become for our clients not only objects of transference, but live, breathing, loving, attractive people. Our clients' friends and spouses pale in comparison to our unconditional acceptance and professional relationship-building skills. We are rarely angry, irritable, short-tempered, or demanding. Instead we demonstrate only compassion, patience, wisdom, and control. Our clients feel attraction and gratitude. Some people, especially those who may find themselves in therapy, want to show their affection with their genitals.

And so we understand how a client might be motivated to conquer sexually a powerful, attractive model who may also be a reminder of prior unresolved relationships. What then of the temptations felt by the therapist? We also have unfulfilled needs. Our hormones do not differentiate which members of the opposite sex are off limits. So we try to ignore our own needs for intimacy, for sexual contact, for friendship with clients. Many of our clients not only look good to us but feel good to know. They are people not unlike ourselves—motivated to grow. They have been dedicated learners. Some have worked very hard to turn themselves into our pygmalions. They can express feelings fluently, use the language and terms we favor. They have been completely open, sharing, and honest with us. They have disclosed their histories, fantasies, dreams, and desires. And for this dedicated effort, we like many of them a lot.

The consequences of acting on our erotic impulses are obvious. We not only lose our objectivity, but we jeopardize the trust and therapeutic work that has been accomplished. Sexual contact with clients or ex-clients is usually an abuse of trust and power and is always self-indulgent and antitherapeutic. Many of the victims of "therapeutic incest" experience lower self-esteem, sexual dysfunctions, feelings of exploitation, anger, betrayal, and a feeling of mistrust toward other helping professionals that makes them reluctant to seek treatment for their now compounded problems (Zelen, 1985). We know all of this. And that is why we work so hard to restrain our natural (and unnatural) desires.

Other aspects of the therapeutic relationship are less clearly delineated. If Holroyd and Brodsky (1977) report that

6 percent of the therapists they surveyed admit to having had sexual intercourse with clients, and we assume that such activity is probably more pervasive than reported, what percentage of practicing therapists have had other forms of erotic contact with clients?

And then there are grey areas in the restraint of intimacy. Some practitioners restrict their therapeutic activities to their offices, whereas others work wonders in the outside world. The difficulty of maintaining intimacy boundaries increases during field trips, sessions conducted in restaurants, at picnic tables, or on bike rides. The temptation to become involved with clients beyond appropriate limits is more severe. The therapist must exercise incredible self-monitoring, self-control, self-deprivation. The pressure builds.

Restraint

The cumulative pressures from maintaining prolonged one-way intimacy are hardship enough for a professional who also requires liberal doses of approval and hugging. The tension is compounded by other ways a therapist exhibits restraint.

From graduate school onward we are told what things we must not do during sessions with clients. First of all, we are warned not to do too much; it is the client's responsibility to do the work, choose the content, pace the progress, develop insight, and change behavior. Embedded in the admonishment to avoid doing too much to rescue the client is an unwieldy list of more specific negative imperatives:

- Do not express personal opinions.
- Do not take sides.
- Do not be too passive.
- Do not be too directive.
- Do not moralize or let personal values show.
- Do not let your attention wander.
- Do not let clients know how you really feel about them.
- Do not have a vested interest in the direction a client chooses.
- Do not meet your own needs during sessions.

- Do not ask close-ended questions.
- Do not share too much of yourself.
- Do not hide behind a professional mask.
- Be honest, but do not say everything you are thinking.
- Use restraint, but do not be mechanical.
- Be genuine, but do not be too transparent.

Depending on one's training, of course, one's personal list of precautions will vary. There is always a theme of "stifle yourself" juxtaposed with encouragement to be authentic.

We know what happens to children who deliberately withhold their true feelings, repress their unsatisfied needs: they become neurotic, well-disciplined adults. We know what happens to children in a double-bind family where they get mixed messages: they become confused or even crazy. What happens to therapists who experience the same thing?

Self-deprivation comes with the territory. We are trained and paid well to put others' welfare before our own. We are disciplined to diffuse our own desires. "By dispassionately acknowledging our personal needs, we lessen their grip on our actions. More and more we simply observe rather than identify with our motives. It's not so much that we're trying to push them away; denial buys us no peace. Rather, we're loosening our attachment to our motives by stepping behind them" (Ram Dass and Gorman, 1985, p. 193).

In our drive to be therapeutic, we harness self-centered urges. Yet it is hard to tread water with someone on our back without drowning. We can only give so much without needing support in return. And just when we have achieved that miracle of therapeutic love, when we feel comfortable and safe, when we even look forward to the meetings with clients we have grown attached to, it is time to say good-bye.

Termination anxiety in the therapist is elicited by several factors enumerated by Martin and Schurtman (1985). Unresolved separation and fears of abandonment can be rekindled as a profound sense of loss. These feelings are further complicated by the therapist's natural reactions to the client's ambivalence over termination. The clinician may feel guilt, failure, disappointment, sadness, pride, apprehension, hope, jealousy, or relief—all at once. And there is the constant cycle of growing immensely fond of people and then turning them loose.

As the Little Prince tamed the fox through the observation of proper rites and regularly scheduled meetings and became responsible for him, so do we feel love and obligation toward the people whose heart and intellect we first tame and then set free. "You become responsible, forever, for what you have tamed" (de Saint-Exupéry, 1943, p. 88).

Narcissism

Restraining our egos is a challenge many of us will never quite overcome. What with our diplomas, titles, and carefully appointed chambers, it is hard for us not to take ourselves seriously. Such self-centered preoccupation with the image we project to the world is indeed hazardous to our mental health. We become disembodied selves, separated from our feelings and from those of the people we try to help.

In Lowen's (1983) treatise on narcissism he describes the pervasive disease of our time that strikes therapists as well as their clients. A lack of feeling, the need to project an image, the desire to help others in order to exercise power, and arrogance are all familiar symptoms. Lowen further describes the phallic-narcissistic personality, portraying himself and many colleagues in a mold of exaggerated confidence, energy, dignity, and superiority. We do act as though we know what is going on most of the time.

From their study of narcissism, therapists Herron and Rouslin (1984) believe this obsessional defense has its roots in our need for control. The desire to help is masked by self-interest, by power, by competition, by winning approval, and by spoors. Yes, spoors—leaving our tracks behind.

Honestly consider for a moment the real kick you get out of being a therapist—besides the benefits mentioned in the previous chapter. I suspect that deep within my own heart is the desperate need to influence others. I am afraid of dying, and worse, of being forgotten. I feel as though I am in the process of immortalizing myself with every disciple who goes out in the world with a part of me inside them. It is as if I can cheat the terror of death if only I can keep a part of me alive. Does this motive affect what I do in my sessions? Naturally. Does this grandiose self-involvement limit the quality of my work? Of course. Do I feel impaired in my capacity for empathy because of this narcissism? Unfortunately, yes. But I stay safe. "Empathy means that at a level beyond the therapist's control, the patient is influencing him or her, not intellectually but emotionally. This implies, then, that the therapist is vulnerable, subject to experiencing any feelings, intense feelings, uncomfortable feelings, almost against his or her will" (Herron and Rouslin, 1984, p. 117).

To give up our narcissistic stance is to risk a deeper, more terrifying form of self-involvement: to confront the feelings we fear the most. Like most obsessives, we successfully distract ourselves from those things we least wish to understand. We can avoid real intimacy even in our sacred chambers by keeping clients at a distance. We can glorify the influence we have had on clients while denying their influence on us. With casual grace we can sever a two-, three-, or four-year relationship as if we are dismissing a stray dog with a pat on the rump.

We can distance ourselves from pain by retreating deep inside our chairside manner—a few strokes of the chin, a blank stare, a delusion that we have the power to heal. Enter a woman in her mid-thirties who is far from composed. Suffering oozes from her pores; even her tears have tears. She feels hopeless, despondent, deeply depressed. This is her third attempt to seek help in as many weeks. The last therapist she saw for six sessions.

> "What did he say?"
> "I don't know."
> "You don't remember?"
> "I remember quite well. He didn't say anything."
> "He said nothing?"
> "No."

"What, then, did he do during the time you
spent together?"

"He took notes."

"Uh, huh."

"He said thank you when I paid him at the
end."

"Why did you go back if you don't feel he
helped you?"

"He seemed so important. He came highly
recommended. And he seemed so awfully busy. He
had to arrange things even to fit me in his schedule,
and several times he even was interrupted by calls
from people who needed him. I thought maybe if I
waited long enough he might notice me. But he
only seemed to notice himself. It's like he looked
through me, as if I wasn't there. I felt like a bug he
was inspecting. All he did was take notes. Even
when I broke down sobbing he just looked at me
across his desk and kept writing in his pad."

The woman stopped abruptly, peeked out from behind
her anguish. I asked her if she would give me a chance to help
her. She said she was tired of seeing therapists but she would
think about it and let me know. She drove straight home, drew
a bath, ate twelve antidepressants, drank a pint of bourbon, and
slit both her wrists. She died from the chronic indifference and
narcissism of the therapists who refused to see her as a human
being.

Fatigue

In an article on his life-style, one prominent therapist describes a typical day in which his time is so rigidly scheduled
from 7 A.M. to 2 A.M. the following morning that each fifteen-
minute segment of time is meticulously accounted for. Sessions
are run back to back without a break. Meals are inhaled between other administrative, lecturing, writing, consulting chores
and even conversations must be scheduled in advance (Ellis,

1983). Although he defends this inhumane regimen as an "affair of the heart," it could more accurately be described as "a plain old case of neurotic workaholism" that is part of a maladaptive vicious circle (Penzer, 1984).

Time pressures head the list of therapist stressors (Nash, Norcross, and Prochaska, 1984). There are never enough hours to see all the people we need to see, return phone calls, attend meetings, complete paperwork, do outreach, keep up with the literature, eat, sleep, and have a life outside of the office. We are often running behind schedule. There are often people waiting, yet there is always room for just one more client.

Once the door closes and we immerse ourselves in a session, one would think the narrowed focus on a single life and task would provide some relief from the exhausting pace. With distractions and intrusions kept at bay, the rhythm of the day slowed down to the client's heartbeat, we can feel our profound weariness. It is so hard to sit still: our knees ache; our eyes burn. We experience greater risks of lower back pain and circulatory and metabolic disorders than the population at large (Bellack and Faithorn, 1981). After the eighth, ninth, tenth, or eleventh session in a row there is little left but an empty shell.

We get so tired of sitting, of listening, of talking, or thinking. This fatigue comes upon us from a number of sources described by English (1972): when a therapist takes on too much work out of greed to make more money, or out of pride to test one's limits, or out of habit because it is the path of least resistance, or out of control to protect one's territory, or out of fear of confronting the rest of one's life, emotional and physical tiredness will eventually ensue. "It is, of course, a well known fact that one of the principal causes of a psychotherapist's vulnerability to fatigue is his/her own unresolved emotional problems. They tend to distort one's perception of the patient and his or her problems, to overidentify with the patient, and to use the patient for one's own purposes. These misperceptions and misidentifications often result in entanglements with patients, leading to distress and failure, if not to flight and mental illness, including suicide" (Dai, 1979, p. 27).

Griswell (1979, pp. 50-51) notices the times he feels

weary are those when he is blocking some other feeling: "In one session with a client where tiredness tugged at my sleeve, I found a resentment I had pushed aside about this call at the last minute to cancel our previous session. In another, I looked under the feelings of tiredness and got in touch with some sexual feelings I wasn't acknowledging to myself. With another the feelings were ones of danger and the client volunteered that she was feeling self-destructive and not telling me."

Much of the time we urge clients to avoid the excesses of overwork. We caution moderation to reduce stress, fatigue, and mental exhaustion. We teach people to better appreciate their present moments, to live a tranquil existence. We do all of this while exhibiting the same symptoms of the workaholic.

On a more serious note, we show symptoms of overwork when we skip meals or refuse to decline work when we are already overloaded. We neglect family, friends, and, most of all, ourselves. There is so little time to be alone, to think, to feel, to do nothing. Some of us are reluctant to take more than a few days off work because we fear losing income or losing power in the organizational structure. It doesn't take others very long to realize we are replaceable—even if we nurture the illusion we must do everything ourselves because nobody else could do as good a job.

When we are not working we mull over our cases. We consider the direction our clients will head next, the things we did that we wish we had not done, and rehearse plans for the following week. At odd moments we wonder how clients are getting along. Why did they never return? What did we do to chase them away? These people populate our world. We see them more frequently than we see most of our friends. No matter how much we work to preserve professional detachment, no matter how hard we discipline ourselves to push them out of our minds when they walk out the door, we still carry them around inside of us. How could these people not be significant in our lives and loom in our minds when we spend week after week after week discussing the sacred details of their lives?

I feel exhausted; my energy is depleted, just thinking about the burdens we routinely carry. It is strange to think we work so hard while sitting still. Maybe it is because we must remain immobile and attentive that the job is so tiring. If only we could separate ourselves from the chair. If only our existence outside the chair could be as meaningful as the time we spend enveloped within it.

Futility

The business of therapy is not only draining but sometimes futile. In spite of our best efforts to be helpful, in spite of the client's real desire to cooperate, not all the people we work with get better; some get worse. Oh, we can delude ourselves with excuses such as (1) "The client is really changing but won't admit it," (2) "This is part of the resistance/transference/defenses," (3) "You have to get worse before you can get better," (4) "It just takes time, lots of time," (5) "You win a few; you lose a few." But it hurts when we fail our clients, and we do take it personally.

Perhaps *failure* is too strong a word. Still, there are those times when, despite years of treatment, the only apparent changes a client experiences are a depleted bank account. Ellis (1984) claims it is rash if not downright irrational for therapists to believe they can be successful with all their clients. I am certain he is right. We understand that it is beyond our means to help everybody. Yet, such realization does not protect us from the beliefs that "All my interpretations must be profound"; "I must always make brilliant judgments"; "My clients must appreciate my work and be grateful as hell"; "They should work as hard between sessions as I do when I'm with them" (Ellis, 1984).

These demands sound ridiculous if not impossible. Still, there is no surprise more devastating than receiving a Release of Information form from another therapist who is now working with an ex-client of ours. First anger and betrayal appear; then self-doubt sneaks up and builds to a thundering crescendo. If there is a colleague available to complain to, it is likely we will hear a comforting pronouncement: "You were so effective with that client he is afraid to come back to you knowing he will have to change." Sure.

The truth is we are all incompetent some of the time. We just cannot get through to some people because of our deficiencies and limitations. Most of the time we never find out what really went wrong. The client stops coming and does not return calls. In some ways it feels even worse when a client feels strong enough to know she will not let you get through to her; so it is safe to keep coming without the fear of changing. It is no consolation to remind ourselves we get paid whether the client appears to change or not. We still have to deal with that stoney, determined face. We still have to put up with the games, defensive reactions, and stubborn resistance and not take it personally.

There are those clients who will come forever: the passive-dependent personalities who need someone to dish out approval, the narcissistic people who need an audience, the borderline clients who, when they are not bouncing off the ceiling, need someone they can pay to abuse. It seems futile to work with these people because they will barely improve and will never be cured. We measure progress among the severely disturbed population in terms that are less than spectacular. We have the audacity to believe we can change the tide of a person's genetic structure, a family's rigid hierarchy, or stable personality traits that have been there since birth. It is a miracle that we ever make a difference in these clients' lives. And it is not that unusual for us to encounter a force greater than we are capable of counteracting.

It seems futile to try to convince a seventeen-year-old youth that we can offer him an antidote to his lust for excitement that can compete with marijuana. It is similarly hopeless to lure an alcoholic away from bourbon with the promise of greener pastures. It is futile to help an enraged adolescent when his parents sabotage treatment. When an individual jumps right back into his peer group after leaving our office, it is unrealistic to think we can alter his values. We feel futility when we attempt to cure anybody of anything. Nobody wants what we are selling until they find they have no other choice. By then, they will settle for cosmetic changes if they can just buy some time. We can give them what they want—a little relief—but we know that is futile, too.

Isolation

Therapy exists to provide a safe and private haven for people to resolve their underlying problems. Without a guarantee that communications are held in strictest confidence, it is unlikely that any effective helping could be accomplished. To protect the client's right to privacy, secrecy, and dignity, we swear allegiance to our profession's code of conduct with regard to privileged communication. If we do nothing else in treatment, our primary obligation is to respect and protect the confidentiality of information received during sessions.

Naturally, clients appreciate our integrity and our sense of honor. For us it comes as second nature after the training years are over. We would no sooner neglect to guard our own shameful secrets than we would commit an indiscretion that might compromise a client's safety. When talking about our work in any context—with colleagues, client families, friends, and even spouses—we routinely monitor what we say so that client identities are disguised and their secrets protected. This shield serves our clients well, as presumably our prudence protects their desire for privacy. However, like all barriers, it not only prevents things from getting out, it also ensures that other things do not get in.

One of the most meaningful, interesting, and fulfilling parts of a therapist's life is the time spent with clients. At times we may be practically bursting at the seams to tell friends about some prominent citizen we are working with. And yet we can tell no one about the people we work with nor about the details of what we do.

If we run into a client at a social gathering, etiquette requires us to fade into the background unless the client chooses to recognize us. If a client's name comes up in conversation, we must pretend indifference so as not to give away our involvement. It is as if we were conducting secret affairs with fifty people simultaneously! We even arrange our schedules and offices so clients do not accidently meet one another. All of this results in a kind of sanctuary for the people we help and a kind of prison for ourselves.

What are the effects of this compartmentalized isolation on therapists? Maybe it contributes to our feelings of specialness and sainthood. We suffer in silence so that others may be released from pain. We also may become secretive, mysterious, aloof, and evasive when we are not at work, while we continue to struggle to be authentic, transparent, and genuine with clients. We retreat inside ourselves for comfort and pat ourselves on the back for being so professional. Actually we feel like martyrs.

All over the city there are restaurants and bars we cannot feel comfortable visiting because clients or ex-clients work there. At parties we have to monitor closely how much we drink, knowing that getting out of control would sully our reputation. Neighbors watch our children for signs of emotional disturbance so they can substantiate the myth of the crazy shrink down the block. People are constantly asking for advice about what to do with their jobs. Others feel intimidated by their own perception of therapists as mind readers. They will not get too close for fear we can disrobe their insecurities with a casual glance. "Oh you're a therapist. I suppose I should be careful around you. (Giggle)."

So we live in glass houses on display. If clients or prospective clients research our reputations in the community, we hope they will discover we are not only competent professionals but nice people. Because we are being watched, we stay in line and cultivate a consistent image. We watch, listen, speak when we are spoken to, and keep our mouths shut.

Conflict

Police officers do not like to break up domestic fights for two reasons. First, people in the throes of conflict can be irrational and violent toward anyone in their proximity. Second, it is painful and uncomfortable to be around people making complete asses of themselves. Any therapist who does marital and family work gets used to the role of participant-observer in human squabbles. Initially, we make it safe for people to feel at home and to be themselves. Then, we give them permission to say what is on their minds, what is really bothering them. We may even aggravate matters a bit by provoking clients to say what they feel and respond to what has been said. We tell them conflict is constructive, sit back, cross our arms, and duck a lot. Even if such activities are eventually helpful for the client, nobody can convince me that the therapist does not suffer.

There are those therapists who grew up in homes where verbal abuse and active conflict were common and those therapists who never experienced such fireworks. For those who watched their parents fight, it can be awfully uncomfortable being part of other parents' arguments—no matter how much we believe it is therapeutic. For those therapists who lived in relative tranquility as children (or at least where fighting was not a spectacle), it is just as unnerving to observe people acting out their anger and resentments in passionate tirades. About the only thing that is worse is when they turn on us.

There is nothing worse than a client who decides he has been betrayed by his therapist. A client can turn on his therapist for a variety of irrational or justifiable reasons: as a distraction, as punishment, or just as a habit of abusing "the help." We can tell ourselves again and again, "This is not personal. This is not . . . " Yet it still hurts. At best, several difficult sessions must be devoted to working through the anger or transference. At worst, there is the threat of malpractice suits or harassment. Fisher (1985) describes the frequency with which therapists are being harassed by unfounded nuisance suits that leave eternal scars. We help a dependent wife to gain her emotional freedom. She decides to divorce her husband and lives happily ever after. The husband is an attorney and very miserable. Naturally, he blames the therapist for his problems and starts legal proceedings as a way to get even. He calls the licensing board and lodges an exaggerated complaint: "This guy brainwashed my wife. He led her astray, convinced her to divorce me. I think he slept with her, too. I hear he does that sort of thing a lot." A year-long investigation will eventually bring the truth out, but not before the therapist has had to fight for his reputation, defend himself to his peers, and survive the mental anguish of harassment.

We hear horror stories or know of colleagues who are actually stalked by ex-clients or their families. They must change their phone numbers, watch over their shoulders, sometimes even relocate their homes. One psychiatrist had been working with a disturbed young woman for a very short time before her estranged husband repeatedly harassed him by showing up at his doorstep. Even after the psychiatrist moved, he was still tracked down, his privacy invaded, and his life threatened. Another counselor became too informal and friendly with a hysterical client and paid for his mistake dearly. After two years of attempts to discourage the client's professions of love, numerous court orders, phone number changes, and complete silence on the part of the counselor, he still receives six to eight messages per day on his answering machine. Maybe it is not all that surprising that there are such incidences considering that our clients and their families frequently suffer from mental disturbances. By definition, our clients are emotionally immature and behaviorally inept. How can we hope to be around such conflict without some of it wearing off?

What happens to someone who constantly watches other people screaming and arguing? He develops a callous and cavalier attitude and grows desensitized to emotional trauma. Or the therapist becomes one of the walking wounded with a case of battle fatigue. Whenever voices reach a certain decibel level, he involuntarily flinches. Whatever the case, a therapist's tolerance for witnessing conflict and remaining in control of the situation changes—quantitatively or qualitatively. If we have to play King Solomon on the job we sure do not feel like it at home. Let someone else make decisions and run the show.

I personally have great difficulty dealing with people who are mad at me, even when I did nothing wrong. A client owed me money for two years. I wrote a firm letter requesting payment immediately. A message waits on my machine that is loud, angry, incoherent. I guess she had a set-back and will not be paying her bill. A mother calls me every week to complain about what a lousy job I am doing with her son (he is trying to break away from his mother). Whenever I suggest she take her son elsewhere, she becomes even more irate. She will do no such thing. I started this mess so I have to clean it up. "Yes, Mrs. X. Thank you for calling." Another client indignantly cancels all further appointments after learning we have a mutual acquaintance. I call to refer her to another therapist and she acts as if it is part of a conspiracy. A marital case becomes a divorce case, and they act as though it were my fault. An insurance company decides not to reimburse a client; again, it is my fault. And, of course, whenever clients do not get better fast enough it is always our fault.

Money

Therapy is practiced differently in different settings. The clinical approach, the length of treatment, and the methodologies employed will depend, to a large extent, on economic realities. In a community mental health center with a two-week waiting list and funding contingent on the number of new patients enrolled, it is unlikely that psychoanalytic treatment will be all that popular. And, in private practice where a therapist's very livelihood depends on being able to consistently sell one's time by the hour, it is unusual to find someone practicing short-term behavioral therapy interventions. A therapist with a large turnover could require more than 400 new referrals every year just to survive, whereas another clinician can get by quite comfortably with 10 or 12.

We belong to a profession whose members cannot decide whether they are scientists or philosophers, technicians or artists. We cannot agree on whether therapists should be trained in schools of medicine, education, liberal arts, or social work. We cannot agree on whether therapy takes a short time or a long time, whether it ought to focus on the past or the present, whether we should work with what the therapist or client thinks is the problem, or even whether the therapist should talk a lot or a little. And, perhaps most important of all, we cannot decide whether therapy is essentially a profession or a business. Frank (1979) candidly admits that once upon a time he did therapy to help people; now he does it for money. Whereas once helping people was fun; now, it is work. And he is not

ashamed to admit that a part of every therapy hour is spent calculating how much he earned while listening to someone tell
their story.

Monetary issues muddle things a lot. Once upon a time,
the practice of therapy, like that of medicine or law, was a calling. It was less a job or a career than it was a commitment to
helping. There was passion and single-minded devotion to a
simpler world with simpler ideals. Then the baby boomers hit
the job market, and the market tightened up. The image of therapy was transformed from that of a kindly country doctor dis-
pensing advice to that of a consummate professional with computer and psychometric support. Legislators began regulating
the field. Professional organizations mandated appropriate conduct. Insurance companies got into the act, then came health
maintenance organizations and preferred provider plans. Now
competition for customers is the name of the game for many
therapists and mental health organizations.

Now clinicians are caught between images of themselves
as missionaries and behavior that is more characteristic of manu-
facturers' representatives. We feel angry about being unappreciated and underpaid. Sometimes it seems that no amount of
money could fairly compensate us for the aggravation, intensity, emotional turmoil, conflict, frustration. Other times we
feel guilty about being overpaid for doing nothing. In exchange
for spending forty-five minutes listening to someone talk and
then telling them what we think about what they said, we receive enough money to buy ten books or a whole night on vacation. It is absurd. It would almost seem that even with the hardships of being a therapist, we have a great thing going. If only
we did not encounter those clients who push us to the brink of
our own madness.

FIVE ❀❀

Patients Who Test
Our Patience

Some of the perils a therapist will encounter are an implicit part of the job. Just as a construction worker would hardly complain about the heights at which he must work or a soldier would not be surprised to find people shooting at him during war, a therapist accepts the dangers of getting close to people for a living. The difficulty is in contending with some of the people we must get close to.

That clinicians have strong preferences concerning whom they prefer to work with is well known. Most everyone prefers clients who are bright, eager, verbal, perceptive, affluent, and attractive. These clients not only grow quickly, but they can be patient, polite, grateful, and will pay bills promptly. Other therapists may express preferences based on (1) the similarity of previous cases that have worked out well; (2) the probability of dealing with issues that are not personally threatening; (3) the challenge the case presents to learn something new; (4) whether the client can make a day versus an evening appointment; (5) what insurance benefits the client has; (6) whether the case falls within one's spectrum of expertise; and (7) the relative likelihood the client will be difficult to deal with. It is the last point that will be the subject of this chapter.

Countertransference

Perhaps the most thoroughly discussed hazard of therapeutic work is the classical countertransference reactions to problem clients. The manifestations of this therapist distortion —overidentification and overinvolvement—may take a number of different forms. Palmer (1980) describes many of the symptoms that are often elicited in therapists by difficult clients:

- The arousal of guilt from unresolved personal struggles that parallel those impulses and emotions of the client.
- Impaired empathy in which the therapist finds it difficult to feel loving and respectful toward the client.
- Inaccurate interpretations of the client's feelings due to the therapist's identification and projection.
- Therapist feelings of being generally blocked, helpless, and frustrated with a particular client.
- Evidence of boredom or impatience in the therapist's inner world during work with a client.
- Unusual memory lapses regarding the details of a case.
- Mutual acting out in which the client begins living out the therapist's values and the therapist begins acting out the client's pathology.

Countertransference was first uncovered by Freud in his relationships with patients (such as Dora) and colleagues (such as Fleiss and Jung). In a letter to his friend Ferenczi during a period of conflict he revealed that he was not the psychoanalytic superman that Ferenczi imagined him to be, nor had he overcome countertransference (Freud, [1910] 1955). He was to develop these ideas in a paper published a few years later in which he stated that the therapist's personal feelings toward the client are both the greatest tool in treatment as well as the greatest obstacle (Freud, 1912). This belief was later echoed in greater detail by some neo-Freudians who thought countertransference feelings were not simply undesirable complications in the therapeutic process but real assets in the promotion of a true human encounter. Such psychodynamic theorists as Frieda Fromm-Reichmann, Franz Alexander, and Therese Benedek felt that although the analyst's personal reactions to patients could be seriously disturbing to both parties, these dangers could be minimized as long as the analyst had undergone intensive treatment and supervision in his own analysis (Alexander and Selesnick, 1966).

There have been many refinements in therapeutic technique since Freud's day, yet clinicians are still struggling with their feelings, distortions, unconscious reactions, unresolved conflicts, misperceptions, antagonism, and subjective experiences in relation to certain clients. Watkins (1985) classified countertransference responses into several broad themes that encompass oversolicitous attitudes and overprotectiveness in a parental role as well as tendencies to win the client's approval through benign friendliness that jeopardizes therapeutic distance. Quite opposite reactions are also elicited in us when we become punitive and aloof in response to a client's demands and dependency. In extreme cases, overt hostility and verbal abuse arise in a therapist to distance himself from the client's pathology.

The obvious point is that we are hardly the same with all our clients. A brief glimpse at the appointment book reminds us of those people we eagerly await and those we dread. We are friendlier with some clients than with others. Some clients are greeted cordially with an open smile and an offer of a beverage, while others are cooly directed to their places with a reminder of their delinquent bills.

A shallow, vulnerable, anxious, and demanding client shows up for an initial interview. She has a variety of psychosomatic complaints and reports she has seen a score of previous therapists who have treated her with Valium, Triavil, Dilantin, and Thorazine but with little therapy because she fires her doctors before they can reject her.

One psychiatrist describes his intense hostility and disdain toward this client, triggered by his aversion to the way she mistreated her husband and child (Weiner, 1982, p. 78):

> The problem that I, as the therapist, initially failed to identify was easy to see in retrospect as I examined my conscious reaction to this woman. I had felt angry with her, was critical of her, and wanted as little as possible to do with her, hardly an attitude that would stimulate rapport. She probably was aware of my attitude during our first ses-

sion, but, not being entirely certain, brought to my attention my failure to suggest a second appointment. I had wanted to dismiss her with an explanation of her symptoms and a suggestion about medication. She was interested in treatment, but I found it impossible to hear that. To me, her voice had been harsh and grating, her attitude demanding, and her interests deploringly selfish.

Some theorists, such as Weisman (1973) and Cerney (1985), consider intense therapist reactions, when recognized, to be crucial in diagnosing how others probably respond to the client. And it is much easier now to admit to countertransference reactions. There is no longer any shame associated with the confession that we have strong emotional reactions—both positive and negative—toward our clients.

Some Therapist Fantasies

When reactive feelings are ignored, denied, distorted, and projected, both the client's treatment and the therapist's mental health suffer. Herron and Rouslin (1984) urge clinicians to examine their fantasies with clients as a clue to how countertransference may be operating. Whether these fantasies are primarily rescue-oriented, sexual in content, or expressive of rage, frustration, and anger, most therapists entertain fantasies and daydream about many of their clients. The following descriptions of reactions toward clients come from a mixed group of social workers, marriage counselors, and psychologists.

I genuinely love a few of my patients. I mean, I love them as much as I love my sister, my best friend, or my husband. I suppose, in a way, a few of my patients have become my closest friends. I think about them during the day, and when I do, I feel warm inside. I have known this one patient for about seven years and I like her *so* much. I feel sad sometimes that I can only know her as her therapist because I would very much enjoy meeting her for lunch and telling her about my own life.

This guy I've been seeing for a few months is the president of XYZ Corporation. He's got a tremendous amount of power and responsibility. He hires and fires people at whim, and he's let me know that I'm under his scrutiny as well. I think about how great it would be if I help this guy that maybe he would invite me into his company to do work with his people. He's got offices all over the world and I think about traveling from Bangkok to Rio putting out fires.

I work with this one incredibly attractive woman who has a crush on me and we both know it. She wears these outrageously revealing outfits and acts quite seductively. Naturally, I interpreted her obvious attempts to sabotage the sessions, and she has toned down quite a lot. But, sometimes I feel this uncontrollable urge to get down on my knees and stick my head underneath her dress.

I could strangle this guy he's so whiney and complaining. He has everything I despise in other people and myself: passivity, external control, helplessness, incompetence. I know he knows that I don't really like him much. But he's so used to having people not like him that my relationship with him seems normal. I end up feeling like he does—helpless—because he refuses to change. As I listen to him talk in his high-pitched monotone, I idly wonder what creative things I could do to break through his inhibited exterior. I picture myself slapping his face or laughing at him. Then I feel such guilt because I lose my compassion.

I sometimes imagine what it would be like to be married to a few of my clients. This one guy is

just a doll and he's trying so hard to improve himself. He's just my type—strong but self-reflective.
There are times during the week I wonder what
he's doing. I also wonder what he'd look like without his clothes on.

These and other fantasies represent only one narrow aspect of the therapist's phenomenological world, and they are
certainly not typical of the way we think about our clients all,
or even most, of the time. Occasionally, however, such fantasies give us clues to how we are personally reacting to our
clients. Only when we are willing to identify and explore how
we feel about our clients and how it affects our clinical judgment can we ever hope to harness this energy constructively.

Difficult Cases

Among experienced therapists there is some consensus
concerning problem clients. Borderline personalities, socio-
pathic personalities, and those with personality disorders test a
therapist's patience and defenses. The prognoses are poor; progress, if any, is slow; and the therapist is likely to be on the receiving end of manipulation, dramatic and painful transference,
and projective identification.

Masterson (1983) characterizes most clients, and especially those with borderline tendencies, as experts in searching
out and exploiting the therapist's vulnerabilities. In this way the
client is working just as hard to destabilize the therapist as the
therapist may be trying to get to the client. Only by promoting
countertransference reactions in the therapist can the client
ever hope to buttress his own resistance and thereby avoid
threats of intrapsychic conflict.

To illustrate the power of borderline clients, Kramer and
Weiner (1983, p. 72) report on how therapists feel hypnotized
to satisfy their disturbed client's expectations and to act out in
much the same way the borderline client would: "A therapist
says she had an argument with her husband one day and found
herself sulking on her front step, thinking, 'I'll get him by getting a kitchen knife and scratching my wrists.' Startled, she

realized that she might be 'catching' her patient's habitual responses.''

All theorists who have ever written on the subject of borderline clients warn of countertransference issues being crucial to the treatment (Campbell, 1982). The therapist cannot avoid the excessive demands made on her, the dependency, aggression, and attacks that are common. All the usual subtle interventions, such as interpretations, are ineffective. We must reach into our bag of tricks and pull out something that will help the client stay in line and protect us from abuse. Similar dynamics operate with narcissistic, passive-dependent, hysterical, and obsessive clients in that the therapist may find herself unconsciously sucked into the client's ploys and games.

A social worker had been working with an obsessive client for two long years without noticing any appreciable difference in her behavior. The client was staying the same, still ruminating merrily along, but the therapist was slowly deteriorating. He started taking the case very personally, was unresponsive to supervision in which he was cautioned to back off, and eventually dropped out of the field because he could not work through his own fears of failure. The client merely transferred to another therapist in the clinic and began slowly chipping away at his sense of potency. (Incidently, this client had been abandoned by her father and divorced by her husband.)

A few clinicians thrive on the challenge of personality disorders. Other practitioners are remarkably patient and effective with psychotic people or drug abusers or with the intellectually impaired. But for most therapists, several patterns of client behavior are difficult to deal with.

I Got Held Up in Traffic. Resistance, in all its manifestations, is hardly the nuisance and obstruction to treatment that Freud once believed. Whether clients are overly compliant or dramatically hostile, we now understand that they are doing the very best they know how to keep themselves together. We also remind ourselves constantly that missed or chronically late appointments are not part of a conspiracy to make us miserable, but rather the client's attempt to retain some control in a threatening situation. Ideally, clients will stick around long enough and therapists will exercise sufficient patience and will set firm enough limits to allow the resistance to be worked through.

Noncompliance by playing with space and time arrangements in therapy is one of those things graduate students are taught to expect but are nevertheless not prepared to handle effectively. No one likes to be stood up (flashback to adolescent rejection), even if she is being paid for the idle time. Some therapists protect themselves by keeping a favorite novel sitting on the desk so if a client is "held up in traffic," or "the car broke down," or "the meeting ran over," the gap can be happily filled. But I still feel uneasy. And it is irritating to wait for someone even if it is part of the cure.

> "Calm down, your job is to wait for people to cure themselves."
>
> "That's easy for *you* to say. I don't like to be kept waiting. It's disrespectful and abusive."
>
> "Now, now. If the client knew more mature and responsible ways to express anger and resentment he wouldn't be coming to you in the first place."
>
> "I know that. But I don't have to like it. In fact, it's the one part of this job I despise. I'm a punching bag who is supposed to hang suspended, bouncing back, not taking it personally when the client decides to take out on me everything he ever wanted to do to his father, mother, sister, and boot camp instructor."
>
> "That's just the transference. You know . . . "
>
> "What do you mean *just*? What are you—a masochist? You *like* people to play games with your head? You enjoy being deceived, manipulated, and resisted?"
>
> "Yes. I probably do. Or I wouldn't be in this field. You don't mind it as much as you pretend to either."
>
> "True. But a little cooperation would be

nice occasionally. I didn't devote my life to being
someone else's paid servant. I don't like always
being the patient and all-forgiving one."

"Then become someone else's patient."

I Want to Die. Death is the ultimate failure. It is especially tragic when someone takes his own life—not only for the
victim but for those who are left behind. Family, friends, and
those who tried to help experience guilt, responsibility, and re-
gret. For any therapist who has ever lost a client through suicide
there is a special sadness, a vulnerability, and a fear that it could
happen again.

Suicidal clients present a challenge on multiple levels.
Foremost looming in our souls is the pure emotional terror of
being close to someone who is so despondent and desperate that
nothingness seems like a viable option. There was a time in all
our lives when we flirted with hopelessness; it was a time we
would like to forget.

Secondly, we feel an incredible burden of responsibility
in trying to help a suicidal client. There are, of course, risks of
legal repercussions if things go awry. There are also moral obli-
gations to push ourselves beyond our usual limits, to do everything within our power to be vigilant and effective. A mistake
or miscalculation may have lethal consequences. We must make
ourselves available day and night, on call for genuine crises or
lambs crying wolf. Every threat must be taken seriously.

Thirdly, once a risk of suicide is assessed, a different therapeutic machinery is set in motion. Records are documented
meticulously. All clinical staff move cautiously, covering themselves, doing everything according to the book. But it is hard to
be all that therapeutic when handling a client with kid gloves.
Confrontation and deep interpretations are tabled in favor of
mild explorations of feeling. Until the client is once again on
stable ground, most efforts are devoted to simply maintaining
basic life functions while rekindling the will to survive. There is
a tightrope to walk between pushing the client hard enough to
get him off the fence and not pushing him over the brink. The
margin for error is small, and the pressure on the therapist is
profound.

A fourth challenge is in being able to leave the problems of the potentially suicidal client at work. Needless worry will not prevent a tragedy. Therapists who spend their time excessively preoccupied with clients at risk do so more for their own benefit as a distraction and inflation of power than for any useful purpose. We can feel important running around with beepers beeping the siren of despair. We can feel needed when we are interrupted at the most inopportune moments by a nagging voice that asks: "Did you do everything you could?"

How Do You Feel About Me? At one time or another, most clients troll for our affection. They do so as part of the transference to get out of us what they always wanted from another, or they do so because in our role as a model we have the power to dispense approval for those actions that are desirable. Another possibility is quite simply that we are the confidants of people's secrets and they have a natural curiosity to know how we feel about them. Although we may use evasive tactics to deny that we feel anything at all or choose to withhold such opinions as irrelevant, clients well understand the rules of the game.

With seductive clients we find our powers of restraint pushed to the limit. Some of them are determined to have their way. Klopfer (1974) outlines many reasons why seductive clients can be persistent. Conquering a therapist is the ultimate victory, proof that anyone can be corrupted. It is a way the client can regain control of the relationship, win power and approval through means that have previously been successful. It satisfies the desire to flirt with the forbidden and is a way a client can frustrate the therapist just as she has been frustrated by the therapeutic experience. It is a way that two people who feel close to one another can feel closer. Yet it is the best way that a client can confound the relationship, sidetrack the treatment, and prevent further therapeutic assaults.

The therapist's efforts to confront the client regarding the seductive behavior can often lead to further frustration. If the feelings are directly discussed and the therapist gently yet firmly rejects the overtures, the client may feel humiliated and rejected. If transference feelings are interpreted, the client can fall back on denial. Yet, if the therapist attempts to back off

and let things ride for awhile, the seductive efforts could esca-
late. There is no easy solution.

One other part of this problem deserves attention: clients
may behave seductively for other than sexual motives. So often
sexuality becomes confused with intimacy, especially when a
man and a woman are alone in a room. Many seductive clients
do not have the slightest interest in a physical relationship but
would like to establish an emotional one. This problem is just as
common when the client and the therapist are of the same sex.
The client feels she is giving, giving, giving and getting so precious little of a personal nature in return. This perception is
accurate and part of the grand design of things. The client must
therefore exercise considerable ingenuity to find out what her
therapist really thinks of her. Clients may measure the time it
takes us to return their phone calls, how many minutes we will
allow the session to run over, or the frequency of smiles as indications of our true regard.

The therapeutic relationship is a unique and asymmetrical
contractual arrangement in which the therapist retains complete
control to reveal about himself only what he likes. "Thus, from
the therapist's standpoint, the therapeutic transaction provides
intimacy and close personal familiarity without, at the same
time, involving the risks entailed in revealing one's inner thoughts
and feelings to one another" (Henry, Sims, and Spray, 1973, p.
219).

For people who are already insecure about where they
stand in relation to others' esteem, the therapist's detachment
drives them even further away. The clients who get better eventually work all of this insecurity through and become all the
more autonomous because of it. But a few clients consider it
their personal mission in life to get to the therapist—if not
physically, then emotionally.

This Isn't Helping, But I'm Coming Back. There are less
obvious ways to resist treatment, such as the overly compliant
client ("This is so much fun") or the client prone to classical defenses of repression and denial ("I had a happy childhood"),
but the direct challenge to our competence is the most difficult
to stomach. Sometimes these clients are the most diligent as far

as keeping appointments, showing up on time, and at least pretending to do what they are supposed to do to get better. But they keep getting worse, and we may not know why. Oh, we have ready responses to give them:

- You'll get better when you're ready to.
- You're getting better but you just don't know it yet.
- You don't really want the responsibility of getting better.
- This is a normal part of the treatment and an indication we are heading in the right direction.
- This is really frustrating for you.

Deep down inside we are afraid to admit the naked truth: we do not know what we are doing with this client, and we cannot figure out why the client keeps coming back to remind us of our ineptitude. Certainly the key to the puzzle is what the client does get out of returning to the sessions without any apparent gain. Beneath the surface lies the client's hidden agenda.

For ninety consecutive sessions Brenda would enter the office just as the second hand crossed the twelve. She always paid in cash, crisp twenty-dollar bills, which she insisted I count. Each week she would take her place, look up, and sneer. Her opening remark, cutting and cynical, would usually send quivers up and down my neck: "Well, as you probably expect, I'm still not feeling very well. I know I'm a fool for coming here every week, paying you my good money to listen to you pretend you care if I live or die. We both know you're in it for the bucks, but God do *you* look foolish sitting there acting like you know all about me. You don't know shit. When are you going to give up and give me the boot?"

Suddenly one day, just as I dreamed it would be, her facade came tumbling down, leaving behind a quivering, vulnerable human being. I honestly do not think it was anything specific that I did—unless you count ninety consecutive sessions of waiting for her to make the first move. She later explained that after all that time she was just waiting until she felt she could trust me.

As long as these clients can keep us off balance, we will

not be able to get close to them. Since they are used to functioning in antagonistic-affectionate relationships, even our disdain does not disturb them in the least. Their only goal is to keep us in line until they decide they are ready to give up the verbal combat. In the meantime it is kind of fun for them to ridicule this symbol of wisdom.

Sometimes client resistance is a figment of our imagination. The problem lies not with what the client is doing to avoid our well-meaning help but with something in us that is interfering with our being more patient, forgiving, and accepting.

Um. Uh. No. One of the basic rules of therapy is that the client talks. When that convention is broken, all else becomes chaos. Occasionally we do work with people, often children, who are not all that verbal, who answer questions in monosyllables if they answer at all, who are uncertain and indecisive, and who can outwait us. We can try any trick in the book—staring contests, interrogations, monologues, card tricks—and we will still end up with virtual silence. With children it is easier because there are still many nonverbal options in the ways time can be spent constructively.

With overly passive or withdrawn adults, a single hour can last years. I think the clock actually slows down—if not downright stops—when these people enter the room—something in their hormones must impede time. We feel, at first, like vaudeville entertainers trying to get a laugh. We could sing, dance, probably do a striptease, and the silent client would watch indulgently.

> "So what brings you here?"
> "Not sure."
> (Kick in active listening.) "You're feeling uncertain and confused."
> "Uh huh."
> (Wait him out. Silence for four minutes.)
> (Active listening again.) "It's difficult for you to talk here."
> "Uh huh."
> (Try again. Reassurance.) "I, uh, mean with

a complete stranger most people find it hard to get
started."

"Yes."

(Open-ended questioning.) "Can you tell me
a little bit about what is bothering you?"

"My mother."

(Persistence.) "That *is* a little bit. How about
some details?"

"She doesn't understand."

Finally. A breakthrough! The session will drag along at its
own interminable pace. Once there is a hint of feeling, an opinion, a concern, we slowly and determinedly explore its shape
and form, build and connect previous disclosures. Eventually we
help these people to open up more. But it takes so much work.

Equally difficult is the client who talks incessantly but
rarely says much and never listens. These clients also have the
power to slow down the clock. They have been compulsive talk-
ers for so long that they are virtually impervious to interrup-
tions, confrontations, snoring, gags—everything but fire alarms.
Some of these folks eventually find their way into Congress, but
the rest end up in therapy because nobody else can stand to
listen to them.

Occasionally, when they draw a breath, take a drink, or
pause to write a check, they will let the therapist talk for a minute—even a few minutes if she can talk fast—but the client will
only continue with the monologue after this interruption.
Amazingly enough, at the start of the next session the client
will remember exactly where she left off and will continue as
if the week lasted but a moment. Naturally, the client's intent is
to prevent hearing anything that might be unpleasant. Eventually, with patience and persistence, we can get the client to
change once trust is established.

With the silent or excessively verbal client, the therapist is
required to do more, which is to do less. The more we attempt
to manage and control the sessions, the longer the obstructive
behavior will continue. We can well understand this intellectually but may still be unable or unwilling to restrain our im-

pulses to control. To sit with someone hour after hour after hour, and really be with him, while he is off in his own world is a herculean task.

But I Don't Have a Drug Problem. Substance abusers are among those clients who improve only as long as they are in the office. Once they leave, they resort to past habits of getting high to avoid their pain. We face an uphill battle, since therapy can never compete with the instantaneous pleasure that a good drug can provide.

It is hard enough to counteract the effects of past trauma and the usual defensive reactions. Once the ploys of a skilled alcoholic or drug addict are added to the scene, the therapist who really thinks he can make a difference before the client is ready may end up an addict himself. In addition to the abuser's denial that he has a drug or drinking problem, to all of his manipulation, deceit, and sneaking around, are the physiological effects. This client is probably physically addicted, psychologically dependent, and may be experiencing some deterioration and memory loss. The need to escape is much stronger than the need to understand. Avoidance wins over confrontation.

Substance abuse counseling and Alcoholics Anonymous emerged as specialties largely because traditional therapy was not working with the chemically dependent client. As long as she has her Valium, cocaine, or wine to ease the emotional discomfort and pain, she has very little incentive to work on the underlying problems.

Even a relatively harmless drug like marijuana can effectively sabotage any attempts a therapist may make to help a client take constructive action. As long as the client can stay high, locked in his room watching television and munching popcorn, he is not going to be very motivated to do anything that requires much energy.

Clients with drug and alcohol problems who are unwilling to admit their dependency typify the kind of work that can be incredibly frustrating for the therapist. Since the likelihood of success is minimal, the therapist's own feeling of impotence may reflect the client's powerlessness.

Sorry to Bother You at Home. The fastest way to get any

therapist's personal attention is with a 3 A.M. panic attack. It is hard to say what actually precipitates the late night phone call, because by the time we are fully awake we are already five minutes into the conversation. The gist of it is: (1) Did I wake you up? (2) Sorry to bother you. (3) You said I could call if I needed to. (4) This is kind of an emergency.

Phone calls at home, one of an array of devious ploys common to the borderline client, are irritating but unavoidable. Those who are severely depressed or prone to panic need to have the reassurance that they can call if they absolutely have to. But the therapist should effectively communicate that such an option should be the last resort. Two or three calls per year are probably not a nuisance. Anything more than a few per year may be considered a form of cruel and unusual punishment.

Dealing with Problem Patients

A significant number of us probably entered the profession because we like to be needed, to have people depend on us. It is therefore ridiculous for us to complain when clients exhibit exactly those qualities of neediness, dependency, helplessness, and manipulation that they came to us to cure. We must expect a certain amount of intrusion, of having people smother us with their demands and even invade our lives with their late night cries of anguish. We should not be surprised at the lengths a disturbed person will go to get the attention they equate with love.

Several principles should be followed in dealing with any problem client:

1. Determine whether the problem is with the client or with us. In many cases it is our own impatience and need for control that leads to unnecessary struggles and conflict.
2. Respect the purpose and function of resistance and client defenses. It is safe to assume that the client's irritating or manipulative behavior has served him well for quite some time. The fact that we are feeling annoyed and off balance is evidence that this behavior is working with us as well.
3. When feeling trapped, follow the principles of the "reflec-

tive practitioner" that allow a scientist, an architect, a man-
ager, or a therapist to restructure a problem in such a way
that a different set of actions is possible.

4. Do not try to cure the incurable. It is necessary for us to
   accept our own limits and share with the client the responsibility for the success of treatment.

All of the client patterns presented in this chapter make
our lives more difficult, but more challenging. The most important key to preventing boredom and burnout, to surviving in the
field with the minimum of negative personal consequences, is to
do only what we can—no more and no less.

SIX

Boredom and Burnout

Of all the problems a therapist will encounter—from someone who wants to jump out a window to someone who is trying to jump out of his skin—none is more difficult than the challenge to stay energized towards one's work. If burnout is caused by an overload of stimulation, then boredom is caused by its absence—at least in terms of subjectively perceived experience. Both involve a discrepancy between what one is giving and what one is receiving. The first part of this chapter will discuss the phenomenon of therapist ennui and tedium; the following section will cover overstimulation, emotional exhaustion, and a broken spirit. In both boredom and burnout the clinician experiences a loss of motivation, energy, control, and direction. These conditions, if left untreated, can become chronic and incurable.

About Boredom

Boredom involves a loss of interest and momentum, either temporarily or chronically. Although it is a state of incredible discomfort, it also serves to rest the mind and spirit to give them time to rejuvenate (Sinclair, 1982).

People have quite literally died of boredom, and perhaps an intolerance for sameness leads others to the fireworks of madness. Boredom is nature's way of saying: "Get back to work!" If people felt content with staleness and with doing nothing productive, our species would die. We have instinctual urges to procreate and preserve our gene pool, to protect and

83

provide for our offspring. And we have urges and ambition to have more, more, more of what we already have—not because we need new things, but because of that voice within us that protests against contentment.

Kierkegaard (1944) believed boredom to be the root of all evil. He was the first to recognize both its motivating and its destructive nature. Boredom creates a void that is frequently filled with reckless thrill seeking, consumerism, and drugs. When a therapist is bored, she is most vulnerable to the hazards of the profession previously enumerated.

When work becomes routine and predictable, when stimulation is minimal, when a person dislikes her own company and that of others, boredom will seep in to motivate some action. It is less a condition than a way of viewing the world.

Boredom can be caused by a collapse of meaning (Healy, 1984). Once upon a time there was a therapist who wished to save the world. He had a diploma, a jacket with patches on the elbows, a leather chair, and the best of intentions. Then he discovered that most of his clients did not want his help and the rest of the people in the world went to someone else. Day after day he said the same things to his clients and they said the same things to him. He said, "If you're so miserable why don't you change?" They said, "I can't." So time went on. His elbow patches became frayed. And so did his patience.

He began to feel more and more confined by his leather chair; by this time it had lost most of its stuffing. Even the diploma had yellowed. And his clients stopped saying "I can't" and started saying "I won't." This did not seem to him to be much progress. His prison walls grew closer.

"If it's prison we're in, we righteous helpers, what are we charged with? Breaking and entering with the intention of doing good? Felonious assumption of personal responsibility? Selling water by the river? And what is our defense? Early conditioning? They made me read *Helper Rabbit* every night until I was eight, your Honor. In my house, the cry 'Help!' was an order not a plea" (Ram Dass and Gorman, 1985, p. 125).

Boredom has its benefits, as sensory deprivation experiments will attest. Those athletes who run or swim or bike in ultramarathons for eight hours at a time can also testify to what endless repetition can teach. A long-distance swimmer reports: "You drop into a hypnotic trance. It's not only that you're doing something for eight or ten or twenty hours, but also your communication is cut off. I wear tight rubber caps on my ears; I can't hear very well at all. The goggles just fit over my eyes and I'm turning my head 60 times every minute, so I don't see very much. I don't have time in that eighth of a second that the breath lasts to focus on anything. A lot of childhood and sexual images go through my mind—quick, dreamlike flashes that come like a picture on a movie screen. When I've finished a swim I feel like I know myself better" (Smith, 1976, p. 48).

While we are bored there is time "to strip away our character armor, shed layer after layer of imposed motivations and values, and circle closer to our unique essence" (Keen, 1977, p. 80). It is a time to stand naked and confront one's pain without distractions or diversions. World-class runners are able to simulate a perfect state of boredom in their quest for optimal performance. They refuse to retreat into fantasy when the pain becomes intense but instead stay with the discomfort and pain: "I not only pay attention to my body as I run, but I also constantly remind myself to relax, hang loose, not tie up" (Morgan, 1978, p. 45). Pounding the pavement, mile after mile, hour after hour, they concentrate only on the nothingness of where they are—the placement of the foot, the pace of breathing, the swing of arms. They excel because they are willing to put themselves in that place where there is nowhere else to escape to.

Therapist Vulnerability to Boredom. The experience of boredom is, in part, affected by a person's conception of time. Those who are clock-watchers (as therapists tend to be), who are constantly aware of how time progresses, are going to find themselves waiting more often for things to happen. Their involvement in life is going to be regulated by what the clock dictates. The nature of a job that requires the precise timing of a conversation to the minute, with frequent (five to ten times per hour) checks of the clock, is going to make therapists much more vulnerable to the subjective flow of time. Since boredom is most likely to occur when time seems to slow down, clock-watchers, by inclination and training, are going to be more aware of this phenomenon.

Where people have a radically different conception of time, in Latin American cultures, for example, boredom is experienced with less frequency. Ask a person on the street what time it is, and rather than hearing the precise voice of a person with a digital watch, "8:48," you will hear a gravelly and unconcerned "about 9:00" with an accompanying shrug to indicate "what's the difference?" In Latin cultures there is a great respect for the present and less concern for the future. Nothing is more important than what you are doing now—talking to a dog, finishing a conversation, watching one of the frequent car accidents. Therefore, regardless of what the clock says, whatever you are currently involved in should not be rushed. Time will wait; and if it will not, who cares?

At the most prestigious university in Peru, I taught a seminar for the country's most motivated and talented students. Naturally, I was excited by this opportunity and, as is my habit, arrived a few minutes early to orient myself to the classroom (I had been bored waiting in my office staring at the clock). The class was to start at 9:00 A.M. and at precisely this time I found myself standing before a room full of empty chairs. At 9:20 the first student arrived; by 9:35 the room was half-full. Confused but infuriated I began my lecture only to find it interrupted every few minutes by another student casually strolling in. By 10:30 I had planned a break and with great firmness, in careful and clear Spanish, I urged them to be back at 10:40. I knew I was in for trouble when I noticed nobody was wearing a watch. By 11:15 we were again assembled, which left me forty-five minutes to cover three hours worth of material. I stopped a student after class to find out how the best and brightest ever learn anything if they are never in class. She looked at me as if I were a pitiful creature and patiently explained that it is the way of her country for students to learn in any form that was spontaneously available. She, for example, was late to class because she was involved in a heated argument with another student over some obscure theory. Did I honestly expect her to abruptly end the discussion just to rush to my class? My own experience with boredom came to an end at that moment (at least while I was living in Peru). Thereafter I was taught by my students to appreciate whatever is happening at the moment. To interrupt the flow by consulting a watch is sacrilege.

Csikszentmihalyi (1975) observed exactly this phenomenon while researching the experience of boredom among rock climbers, surgeons, chess players, and dancers. If one of these individuals interrupted his activity to consider time, the intense enjoyment, the immense sensation of flow ceased. Flow occurs only when there is a heightened concentration without effort, when the activity is perfectly balanced between boredom and anxiety, when there is a loss of time and space so that the person becomes that activity. Boredom is impossible for those who are so totally involved in what they are doing that they become that action:

A rock climber: "You are so involved in what you are doing [that] you aren't thinking of yourself as separate from that activity . . . " (p. 39).

A chess player: "When the game is exciting, I don't seem to hear nothing—the world seems to be cut off from me and all there is to think about is the game" (p. 40).

These descriptions are hardly unfamiliar to us. When we are totally focused in a session, when our words flow forth, when we become the client, when we forget about the room or the chairs, when there is an absence of thought, we experience flow. The session ends too quickly. And we have done our best work even if we cannot recall what we did.

But when we lose the sense of challenge, when we think we know where things are going, boredom infects us. Time seems to stand still. We feel embarrassed by the number of times we have looked at the clock. After planning our dinner menu in our head, calculating our income to date, going off into fantasy land, we notice with a start that someone is talking: "What are *you* doing here? Why don't you go home?"

It is the repetition that is so difficult to tolerate, not only in the similarity of client complaints, but in the therapeutic messages we relay. Rational-emotive therapy, for example, can be infuriatingly repetitive in its execution. Even Ellis (1972, p.

119) admits: "I have seen myself at times doing the same thing over and over with clients and have recognized that this is a pain in the ass, this is something I don't greatly like."

Burton (1972) points out that therapists have a particularly difficult time dealing with boredom and so chose a lifestyle that permits a variety of tasks, allows them to get to the heart of problems quickly, and grants them the opportunity to work with very interesting and very strange people. He claims therapists seldom feel bored because they get to hear such titillating secrets from clients who try very hard to be entertaining. The people who march through our offices are indeed unique and individual, yet after years of practice, so many of the voices sound the same.

> A marriage counselor: "If I hear another husband say he'll do anything to save his marriage but he doesn't have time this week to schedule an appointment . . . "
>
> A psychiatrist: "They all want drugs. They come in prepared to do a song and dance showing how sick they are and hoping for relief from some magic pill they think I'm hoarding."
>
> A psychologist: "I've done over 4,000 Wisc-R's in the last several years. I do them in my sleep. Sure every kid is different, but the damn questions never change."
>
> A social worker: "I don't know how many visits I've made to the homes of abused children. It's always the same. I go in, interview the parents who swear the kid slipped in the bathtub, then admit maybe they did try to teach her a lesson but they'll never do it again. 'You've got to teach these kids they can't walk all over you.' 'Yes, Mr. Walker, but your daughter is eighteen months old. What did she do, *crawl* all over you?' They never get the point and they'll never change. The kid will go to a foster home and probably get beaten by someone else. Maybe a long time ago I found this interesting. Now it's just frustrating and boring."

English (1972, p. 95) recounts his experiences with boredom in therapy work: "There have been patients I liked to see and treat and some I dreaded to see, some who amused me, some who bored me to distraction. Some could put me to sleep, and I use the word *put* rather than say I went to sleep on them. Because I would find myself thinking, 'How sleepy I am. When the patient leaves I'll take a nap for sure!' But when he departed the office I couldn't go to sleep for the life of me."

Boredom and the Avoidance of Risks. On one end of the continuum is a therapist steeped in boredom—demoralized, dissatisfied, restless, and weary; on the other end is someone who has become timid, irresolute, and fearful of taking risks. Just as change in clients is stymied by a reluctance to act differently or experiment with new modes of being, so, too, do some therapists tend toward safety, security, and predictability at the expense of growth.

Therapists can avoid constructive risking in a number of ways. Here we are not talking about reckless thrill seeking but rather about those occasional opportunities to take an unknown route and end up in a very different place. Reluctance to expose oneself to hazard and danger, unless the perceived gain seems worth the potential loss, is sensible. But much more than the concern to protect ourselves from needless jeopardy is a pathological avoidance of risk that may reveal us to be impotent, ineffective, or inadequate. When one is secure and comfortable, it takes some real incentive to venture out into the cold. We may therefore be just as guilty as everyone else of postponing action until it becomes absolutely necessary and of avoiding the unknown when it is at all possible.

Therapists who play it safe in their work may remain basically satisfied with their moderate gains. They will do just enough to get the job done, but not enough to ever produce dramatic results. Under the excuse of protecting their client's welfare, they will avoid confrontation and conflict, preferring instead to move at a pace consistent with the client's own tolerance for boredom. They will wait and wait, knowing that waiting has its therapeutic value, and that most clients will get better on their own or in spite of what we do. They will say only what they have said before. They will do only what has been tried before. Any departure from the formula must be preceded by a consultation of the works of their favorite authority.

Certainly it is neither appropriate nor helpful to advocate risky therapeutic interventions to appease some restless spirit in the therapist. On the contrary, those who are able to satisfy their needs for stimulation and excitement in their personal lives have no interest in using their clients as guinea pigs in experimentation for its own sake. Therapists, in fact, have an obligation to protect people at risk from exposure to unnecessary dangers. But there are many ways a clinician may safely and responsibly try new intervention strategies without jeopardizing the client's safety.

Solutions to Boredom. Although boredom is an inevitable if uninvited guest, it need not stay long. Yet when the clinician feels apathetic and helpless it may become a permanent resident. Sometimes, despite a fervent desire for renewal, boredom nevertheless hangs on.

The primary cure for boredom in therapy is to focus on the uniqueness of each case, the individuality of each client, and the opportunity for growth in every encounter. When our minds function routinely and interventions have become mechanical, we experience tedium. When I catch myself feeling blasé about the real magic that is transpiring in my involvement with a client, I make a deliberate shift in my perception. If I first shift my position in the chair and concentrate on my breathing and on my posture, if I go back to the basics I learned as a student, I find something wonderful takes place. The client becomes more special, her words carry more power, the whole experience becomes energized. I can feel the new energy, and so does the client. As she notices my renewed interest, she begins to feel and act more interestingly, not to entertain me and release me from my boredom, but because I value our time together more. She begins to believe she is more exciting. The changes are, at first, very subtle: I forget to watch the clock and the session runs over.

Another practitioner relates his own strategy for avoiding staleness in his work: "I have never been bored . . . I consider myself very fortunate to be doing such interesting work, particu-

larly when I can experience a degree of falling in love with a patient. This is not a threat to my marital commitment but rather
is a further installment on the resolving of my romance with my
parents and my siblings. When I can no longer fall in love with
patients to some degree, I will be approaching the end of my
vitality as a therapist" (Warkentin, 1972, pp. 258-259).

Other therapists successfully immunize themselves against
boredom by taking on challenging cases that do not permit a lax
attitude. It also helps to be under the supervision of someone
who helps keep us off balance, humble, and comfortably confused. Boredom can thus be kept at bay by working consciously
and deliberately to keep things fresh, and especially by looking
for meaning in the things we do.

About Burnout

Burnout is the single most common personal consequence
of practicing therapy. No matter how skilled a practitioner is at
avoiding other occupational hazards (including boredom), there
will be some period of time—a day, a week, a month, or all eter-
nity—in which serious consideration will be given to leaving the
field. Perhaps it will be one of those days when successive "no-
shows" combine with an irate phone call from an irrational
parent. Or maybe one of those weeks in which you discover
that the supervisor you liked has moved on and the colleague
you did not like has just been promoted over you to that position. Or one of those months in which your tires are slashed by
an ex-client you thought you had helped and your ego is repeatedly slashed by peers trying to undermine your authority,
referral sources who have lost confidence, a supervisor who
feels threatened by your superior intellect, and clients who will
no longer return your phone calls.

The question, then, is not who will experience burnout
but how long the next episode will last. It is the nature of the
human condition in general, and the therapist condition in particular, to experience ebbs and flows in life satisfaction. Ours is
a very emotional business with many highs and lows. Sometimes
we can feel as close to being a god as any mortal can approach—

powerful, elegant, graceful, wise—and other times we can feel so totally inept we wonder how we can be allowed to continue to practice. No matter how many people we have helped and cured, deep down inside there is a sickening feeling we will never be able to do it again. For the life of me I do not really know what I did the last time. And when a new client comes in, sits down, presents his case, and then expectantly waits for my assessment, there is always a minute of panic in which I stall and think to myself: "I don't have any idea what's going on, nor do I have the foggiest notion of what is going to help this gentleman." Then, I take a deep breath, jump in, and say something, anything, if only: "I don't know yet what is happening, but I'm sure we'll figure it out together."

Symptoms of Burnout

A number of fairly specific behavioral indices of acute burnout have been described by several authors. The following discussion of the symptoms of, causes of, and cures for burnout was inspired by input from Freudenberger (1975), Bach (1979), Edelwich and Brodsky (1980), Pines, Aronson, and Kafry (1981), and Maslach (1982). Because burnout is often a disorder of rapid and dramatic onset, it is easy to recognize. The symptoms that follow are the clearest indications of an incipient problem.

• There is a general unwillingness to discuss work in social and family circles. When queried by friends about what is new at the office, the therapist's eyebrows rise, shoulders shrug, but nothing comes out. In fact, the therapist, if she makes any response at all, may snort and then use all her therapeutic skills to deftly change the focus to someone or something else.

• There is a reluctance to call the office or answering service for messages and a resistance to returning calls. It is as if there could not possibly be any message waiting that is worth getting excited about. In his most pessimistic state, the burned-out therapist may think that a message could bring only one of three possibilities: (1) someone is cancelling an appointment at the last minute, leaving a gaping hole in the therapist's schedule during the middle of the day, (2) a new referral has called and wants to be squeezed immediately into an already overloaded week, (3) a life insurance agent has called to talk to the therapist about his inevitable death.

• When a client does call to cancel, the therapist celebrates with a bit too much enthusiasm. Dancing and singing in the hallway is a dangerous sign of advanced deterioration. Whispers under one's breath such as "Thank God!" and other feelings of relief are certainly more socially appropriate but equally indicative of professional dread.

• One of the best clues to burnout in a therapist is when several clients complain of similar symptoms. When there is a rash of complaints about hopelessness, frustration, pessimism, and doubt in the therapeutic process, the clinician may silently be in agreement. Since clients resonate our faith and beliefs, they also sense and imitate our despair. A frustrated and unmotivated therapist does little to promote growth in his clients. It is hard to imagine that his clients are going to do more than go through the motions of their treatment. If they improve, it will be largely in spite of their therapist rather than because of his help. In fact, some clients will get better just to escape the punitive drudgery of their sessions.

• Daydreaming and escapist fantasy are common. During sessions, the therapist's eyes are inadvertently drawn to the window or door. It takes constant vigilance to stay with the client. Yet, in spite of these good intentions, the mind drifts away to some other place and time. During idle periods, the escapist thinking continues as the therapist imagines herself rescuing princes in distress or lying on a beach in Eleuthra.

• The alarm clock is less a signal to begin the day than an order to resume one's sentence. There is reluctance to get out of bed, and excuses to avoid getting started abound. During the day the therapist functions at half-speed and is lethargic, apathetic, disconnected. Much time is devoted to coffee breaks and ploys to stall action.

• As in all instances of prolonged stress, therapists are prone to anesthetizing themselves with self-prescribed medications. In some cases legal drugs like Xanex and Valium are used with regularity. More frequently, stressed therapists resort to abusing the substance of their choice: marijuana, alcohol, and, for those who are more affluent and upwardly mobile, cocaine.

• Cynicism is manifested in a number of ways. To colleagues and friends, the therapist may make a number of deprecating remarks about clients, ridiculing them for their weaknesses, joking about their helplessness. And the therapist may find a commentary running through her head during sessions: "If you only knew what a fool you look like," "That's what *you* think," "You are so boring no wonder your wife left you," "I don't care what you do, what are you asking me for?"

• Sessions lose their spark, their excitement, their zest and spontaneity. There is very little laughter, little movement. The room feels stagnant. Voices become monotones. There are lots of yawns and uncomfortable silences. Sessions end early.

• The therapist falls behind in paperwork and billings. Progress notes, fee sheets, treatment plans, and quarterly summaries pile up. During the best of times such chores are handled with less than joy; the burned-out therapist may spend more time complaining about the forms to be completed than actually completing them. Management intervenes to slap the therapist's hand, often with other punitive measures to enforce compliance to organizational rules. The therapist eventually capitulates—but with a cursory effort designed to merely play the game.

• During leisure time there is a distinct preference for passive entertainment. Watching television is easier than getting out in the world to do something. "I'm so tired of having to be responsible for people's lives I want someone else to take charge of mine." "I don't feel like doing much tonight."

• The therapist is so emotionally tied to his work that an active social life is completely precluded. He has difficulty relinquishing control, feeling he must do everything himself. He experiences excessive internal pressure to succeed and an overidentification with his clients to the point of losing his own identity.

• Last, but hardly least, the therapist is reluctant to explore the causes and cures of his burned-out condition. Rather than having to make needed changes or confront the emotional difficulties that are blocking satisfaction, he prefers to make excuses and criticize others for the problem. Much of what a therapist does is interrupt this destructive cycle in others; thus, the final symptom of burnout is an inability or unwillingness to apply one's therapeutic wisdom to oneself. There is probably some ironic justice in creating so devastating a punishment for those who would practice therapy in a spirit of hypocrisy and self-neglect.

Causes of Burnout

Depending on one's immunological system, recuperative powers, and work environment, therapist stagnation can either be a temporary nuisance or a tragic flaw that requires a career change. Several influences determine the extent and duration of this occupational and personal crisis.

Predisposing Factors. It is the nature of the human life cycle to experience periods of relative calm alternated with spurts of disorientation and subsequent growth. Freud, Erikson, Piaget, Havighurst, Kohlberg, Levinson, and Loevinger have documented how development proceeds according to an orderly sequence of stages that build on prior adaptive experiences. In the career of a therapist, as well, there are predetermined stages of growth that are facilitated by such variables as formal training, critical incidents, exposure to theories, mentors, and experiences. According to a developmental conception of occupational growth, then, certain predictable "hot spots" will emerge. Therapists are most vulnerable during life-cycle transitions, during periods of accelerated metabolic changes, and after decade-long intervals in between theoretical changes.

Some therapists are at risk not only because of developmental evolution but because of certain personality characteristics. Those with a low tolerance for frustration and for ambiguity, a high need for approval and for mandatory control, and rigid patterns of thought are going to be in for greater turbulence. One social worker, for example, has been practicing orthodox psychoanalysis for twenty years. He subscribes to all the appropriate journals, attends conventions religiously, and is proud of the fact he has not changed his style since he completed his own analysis decades previously. He resists change even within his sheltered professional circles and scoffs at ego psychology or Jungian analysis as too revisionist. He actually does very little in his sessions, although he can explain all the fascinating things that are happening to a colleague for hours. He is often frustrated because he sees little progress in his clients and receives so little feedback from them concerning how they feel towards him.

The seeds of self-destruction may first be sown, if not fertilized as well, in graduate school. Therapists get themselves in trouble with unrealistic expectations and unreasonable goals. No matter what the textbooks and professors say, you are not going to cure schizophrenia by reflecting feelings, and you are not going to wipe out chronic depression by disputing a few irrational beliefs. Naive beginners enter the field prepared to conduct neat, elegant, organized therapy in ten sessions or less with people who will change fast, pay lots of money, and be exceedingly grateful. It takes several years for them to realize that some clients will always be the same no matter what you do; you will never get rich or famous being a therapist; and most of the time you will be unappreciated and overworked.

Bureaucratic Constraints. There are factors within most organizational structures that may make for efficient operations, happy boards of directors, and balanced budgets but are hardly conducive to staff morale. Paperwork is just one example of a product that pleases funding and accreditation agencies but drives clinical personnel up the wall. For every session of therapy that is conducted, the therapist may often spend fifteen minutes describing in sickening detail what the client talked about, what interventions were used, how that particular session contributed to the overall treatment goals, and how the client felt after he left. In some settings all this material must be repeated again and again for summaries, insurance forms, case reports, and departmental files. While some consider noncompliance with this organizational regime as an indication of passive-aggressive behavior or burnout, others have the opinion that only anal-compulsive therapists who hate their clients would ever devote much quality time to producing forms that get filed away.

Some mental health agencies, hospitals, social service departments, universities, and clinics are also notorious for their political wars. Power struggles are waged not only among department heads and within the administrative hierarchy, but especially among the different professional groups. Psychiatrists, social workers, family counselors, psychologists, psychiatric nurses, and mental health technicians often stick together in their respective groups, each with their own biases toward others. The result of this often intense competition is an environment in which people vie for control, status, recognition, and power. In such a setting it is not surprising that people choose to drop out.

Prejudices, biases, and discrimination only add to the frustration of a clinician functioning in a bureaucracy. Promotions and raises are based less often on merit than on credentials, skin color, and sex. Some therapists give up because they feel their careers are at a dead end. They may be able to continue improving themselves as clinicians and administrators, but there is little they can do to alter their background, their race, their religion, or their sex.

Even the most dedicated and well-meaning practitioner who has successfully avoided all the previously mentioned traps may still find it difficult to resist the contagious effects of others' disillusionment. When the institutional norm is to complain about the food, it is difficult to enjoy a meal. When other staff members complain about how they have been abused by the administration, it is hard to go about one's business as if others care for your welfare. In the worst of circumstances it takes a new recruit but a few weeks to lose her initial surge of enthusiasm.

Emotional Stress. Most of the problems contributing to burnout are centered less around the actual daily work than around the therapist's unresolved emotional difficulties (Dai,

1979). Some professionals invest their egos too intensely in the outcome of their work, an outcome that depends very much on the client's motivation and behavior. Therefore, they may attempt to do too much in the sessions, taking too much responsibility for filling silences, providing immediate relief of symptoms, and generating insight. The more control the therapist takes, the less the client assumes. The more the therapist does, the less there is for the client to do.

This is not to say the therapist is justified in a passive, detached, observatory role that allows the client to flounder aimlessly. Certainly we share some responsibility with the client for planning the content of sessions, providing some input into choices, and gently helping to generate a degree of self-understanding and subsequent action. The problem arises when, out of a personal sense of importance, the therapist feels a genuine, gut-level stake in what the client does and how fast she does it.

Emotional factors enter the picture not only for the therapist who tries too hard but for the one who overidentifies with a client's situation. I do not care how many times I hear a young client cry out in anger and frustration at being teased by his peers, I feel the pain every time. As the little guy goes on to relate the incident of striking out for the third time in front of his heckling teammates, I can feel myself actually shaking. I was one of those kids sent into exile in right field.

Often, the sutures closing up an old wound fail to hold against the onslaught of emotional issues presented by clients. Sometimes the best we can hope for is constant vigilance: "This client is not me. This client is *not* me. I am sitting over *here* in the more comfortable chair. I am being paid to sit here, to listen, to react, but *not* to get into my own stuff."

A final emotional issue worth mentioning concerns those therapists who lack family support for their work. Helping professionals require much nurturance, understanding, and demonstrations of affection. After giving and giving all day long, a therapist can come home with a short fuse and long list of demands. Tender loving care is indicated until he or she returns to the land of the living. This is especially true for women in the field who must often contend with more than their fair share of family and household chores in addition to a full work schedule. Single parents also shoulder a disproportionate burden of financial hardships, car pool, laundry loads, and late nights cleaning house.

Cures for Burnout

The result of many of these emotional factors that contribute to burnout is increased isolation and withdrawal on the part of the therapist. Since it is often difficult for many professional helpers to ask for help, the self-destructive patterns become more entrenched and more resistant to treatment. Nevertheless, several self-administered preventions and cures are often useful.

Do Therapy Differently. The simplest and most direct way to breathe life into unsatisfying work is to either do something else or to do what you are already doing a little (or a lot) differently. The profitable business these days of presenting workshops and seminars attests to the popularity of this particular strategy, even if the effects are short-lived. After an initial surge of enthusiasm upon returning from a workshop or convention, many therapists slip back into the doldrums. A good speaker can be infectious in her spirit, but just as in therapy, unless the participant continues to apply the ideas on a daily basis, regression is likely.

After many years of struggling to sort through the vast array of theoretical orientations, therapeutic technology, and conflicting claims, it feels secure to stick with a proven and familiar recipe. Even if we have no particular objection to learning new concepts, new rules, a new vocabulary, and a new set of skills, to go ahead and learn something new seems to mean, in many cases, condemning the old ways to obsolescence. This is hardly the case, since we always retain those ideas that are still helpful. Nevertheless, until a therapist encounters discomfort of sufficient magnitude, there is going to be considerable resistance to radical change. The key, therefore, is to give oneself permission to change a little at a time, to experiment, and to be more creative.

One psychologist had been giving his clients relaxation exercises with great success for years. He had found a proven formula for creating effective and efficient induction procedures, vivid images, and positive results. His clients were still improving (though less so in recent months), but he was feeling much worse. With all the complaints he made about how stale and boring his work felt, with all the options he considered in giving up behavioral strategies, it never occurred to him to simply change his exercise instructions. He did not have to read them any more, but he did so because he did not trust himself to work spontaneously. An unusual example of rigidity, this case highlights the point that a psychoanalyst need not become a Rolfing specialist, nor does a gestalt therapist need to adopt behavior modification in order to re-energize one's work.

Doing therapy differently means forcing oneself to venture off into unchartered territory where the destination is less well defined. It means joining the client as a partner in the spiritual odyssey. Most of all it means conquering burnout paradoxically by initially working even harder until it no longer becomes work at all.

Teach Others. There is a very good reason why so many professors do counseling as an avocation and why so many therapists teach, and it has less to do with generating pocket money than with rejuvenating one's emotions. Therapists teach not only as a way of spreading the gospel and increasing referrals and their reputation, but as a way of giving greater meaning to their clinical work. When you explain to others what you do, how you do it, and why you do it a particular way, you are forced to think through the rationale for every intervention.

An ex-therapist, ex-professor, and now university administrator still works with a few clients just to keep her skills honed and her perspective fresh. She still fights to teach one clinical course each semester even though it means extra work. She does not receive extra compensation, nor do her superiors approve, since it means time away from her office. Yet she does so for her own mental health: "Teaching helps me to be more honest and self-critical. When I talk about what it means to be a good therapist, it helps me to be more that way myself."

Another therapist teaches a graduate-level course even though it means a night away from home and only a token honorarium: "I usually get stuck with the classes none of the full-time staff want to teach. But I don't mind. It's a way to get to talk to people in the field who are still eager and fresh. It's a privilege and honor to work with the really good students. I'd do it for free. I teach this one techniques class that nobody ever likes—not the professors or the students—because it involves making and analyzing verbatim transcripts. My therapy has changed so much since I started studying the work of beginners who know next to nothing. They use low-level and awkward active listening, and yet they are still effective. Since I started going back to the basics in my own work, I'm surprised to find I enjoy it all over again."

A full-time professor relates the impact of teaching on his clinical work: "Questions drive me nuts! The questions some students ask. . . . Like one wise-ass asked me how do I know any of my clients ever really get better. Maybe they're just pretending. Now this guy had no intention of being profound; he was just being silly. I put him off with some appropriate remark. But then I started thinking, really thinking about the reasons I know for sure that clients really change, not just fake it. The more I thought about it, the better I felt about doing therapy."

Clinicians who do research, give public lectures, publish articles, or write books report similar peak experiences. To teach is to magnify our influence. To teach is to continually evaluate what we do from the perspective of an innocent. We feel greater meaning not only in the single life we help to improve, but in how that life helps us to understand and improve the process of change.

Take Personal Responsibility. In every institution in every city of the world, there are therapists who are relatively immune to burnout. They get a tremendous kick out of making a crying child smile or an adult with a plastic smile cry. They stand aloof from the backstabbing, yet retain their power through their expertise, dependability, and tremendous competence. They take care of themselves and the people around them. They expect honesty and respect from those around them. Even in a closed environment we can choose such colleagues as friends.

Corey (1986) suggests that every practitioner take personal responsibility for preventing burnout and maintaining a high level of vitality. Seeking out enthusiastic colleagues is only one of several practical strategies that might include any or all of the following:

- Assume as much responsibility for your own growth as you try to with your clients.
- Use multiple measures of success in your work, not just the client's explicit gratitude.
- Set limits with demanding clients and colleagues concerning what you are willing to do and what you are not able to do.
- Develop outside interests as a form of renewal—especially those activities that exercise parts of your body and mind that go unused during work.

Confronting the Source of Stress. In many cases job stress results from a specific, identifiable source. The physical environment could be a factor—for instance, sharing space with a coworker. The relationship one has with one's immediate supervisor is another definite possibility. Nothing is more frustrating than an incompetent boss who enjoys having others under his thumb; demands stringent accountability; likes paperwork; sends conflicting orders; invites honest feedback, but only if it is pleasant; and understands very little about therapy. In his first job out of graduate school, a man reports that while he counseled young adolescents in a cubicle without a door or ceiling, his supervisor would listen with her ear to the wall. Every time he would say anything to the child she did not agree with, the supervisor would bang on the wall and yell out "Don't tell him that!" When the startled child and fledgling counselor then continued their conversation in a hushed whisper, another bang would ensue followed by the words: "If you two have to be so secretive you shouldn't be talking about whatever you are talking about." The counselor now works as a salesman.

It is always difficult to confront the source of discomfort; sometimes it seems impossible. Excuses for avoiding a confrontation include: "It's not so bad"; "It's probably the same everywhere"; "Everyone else can handle it." But without taking some risks, nothing will ever change—with clients or with ourselves.

The Impaired Therapist

The psychologically impaired therapist has probably ignored his problems for months if not years. His energy has been depleted and a sense of cynical hopelessness has set in. He will infect many other colleagues as well as his clients before the disease runs its course to retirement, death, or disablement.

To make it easier for therapists to ask for help, a number of state professional societies have organized hot lines for impaired therapists. In an effort to reduce the proliferation of therapists who act out in their sessions as well as to control excessive drug and alcohol abuse among their colleagues, professional therapists stand ready to provide assistance where and when it is needed. We all have a duty and responsibility to promote not only the well-being of our clients and our own mental health but the functioning of our colleagues as well. That boredom and burnout often lead to more severe personal consequences such as depression, drug addiction, suicide, divorce, and the breakdown of professional effectiveness is inevitable. We all entered the helping profession to make a difference in the world. The place to start is with ourselves and then with our peers. By rescuing a single therapist from despair, we can multiply the good we can do by helping one client improve by forty times.

SEVEN ✿✿

Lies We Tell Ourselves

Some of the negative personal consequences of being a therapist derive less from the pressure of clients, supervisors, or work schedules than they do from some form of self-deceit. Buried deep beneath that polished surface of a professional truth-buster may be an intricate web of lies. Most of them are harmless little fictionalizations we are aware of and choose to ignore. Others are buried deeper, beyond our consciousness, embedded within our system of denial, rationalizations, and distortions. There are itty-bitty white lies and big black ones. There are lies that are so obviously untruthful that we do not really consider them designed to dupe anyone.

There are lies all around us—in the charters and policies and procedure manuals of our facilities; in the minutes of the board meetings and public advisory meetings; in the stated purposes of an organization: not only to help people or make the world a better place, but also to make money, to provide tax write-offs, to pay off political favors, to keep a few people's egos or bellies well fed, or to satisfy some bureaucratic imperative.

We live especially with the lies that our clients bring to us every day. The really honest clients do not even pretend to disguise their fabrications. And we humor them as well, lying when we pretend to believe that they had a happy childhood, that therapy is such fun, or that the check they owe us is in the mail.

We live with such incredible dishonesty in client disclosures and reports—some of them unconscious omissions, others deliberate falsifications—that we sometimes forget the rough fit between a childhood memory and its repetition years later after being squeezed through the mind's protective sieve. This distinction between narrative and historical truth totally debunks the myth of the client as unbiased reporter and therapist as unbiased listener. To support this idea, Spence (1982) reviews the process of therapy in which the client relates an unfinished story in finished form, creating meaning, transitions, and completion of memories that are actually quite muddled. More of the historical truth is lost during the process of translating images into words. Finally, the therapist distorts the truth of what actually occurred even more by supplying contextual assumptions to fill in gaps. Since it is difficult if not impossible to ever find out what really happened in a client's life, given the lapses of memory, language, and perceptual accuracy, we become comfortable with a certain level of deception and half-truth. We settle for an approximation of truth, in our clients and in ourselves. The result of this reality, coupled with a mind trained to detect the intricacies of rationalization and intellectualization, is a therapist who lives under the spectre of Truth, Justice, and the American Way. But scratch us and we bleed. We are not all that we appear to be.

Types of Self-Deception

Games Therapists Play. We deliberately cultivate our aura of mystery and omnipotence, not to deceive, but to increase our influencing power. No self-respecting wizard, magician, or any professional for that matter could expect to be effective if he gave away the tricks of his trade. And we have a set of special skills we use to convince the Dorothys in the Land of Oz that we are indeed powerful wizards.

For example, clients are constantly amazed at how we seem to know exactly when the hour is over, as if we had a special internal mechanism to sense the subtle changes of time. After years of practice we are rarely caught unobtrusively glancing at the clock when the client is temporarily distracted.

We disguise our imperfections and lapses as well, believing quite rightly that they would interfere with our image as powerful healers. For example, we have developed an impressive array of options to disguise yawns. As we do not wish the client to know we may feel bored or fatigued, we place the hand in front of the mouth in a pensive pose. Strategically sipping coffee also works quite well.

To counteract the temptation to yawn, another subtle therapist skill is the ability to look attentive during lapses into personal fantasy. We can keep head nods, furrowed brows, and "uh huhs" going at the same moment we are fighting our own dragons. Of course, sometimes we get caught and the client may explicitly test our powers of concentration with: "Do you know what I mean?" That is the true test of the experienced clinician, which brings us to a whole new category of maneuver: What to do when you did not hear what the client just said. Even the most directive therapist will lapse back into her best Rogerian response: "My opinion is really important to you." A knowing, mystical follow-up posture will often help to stall for time until we can come up with a more acceptable response.

To err may be human, but it is not all that noble for therapists whose power may be undermined by mistakes. A series of defensive ploys are often required for slips when, for example, our interpretations miss the mark. We can always backpeddle and redefine the misjudgment as "only a working hypothesis" or "a possible theory," but certainly the client will lose confidence. One clever option is to reluctantly explain that the interpretation was actually a paradoxical maneuver specifically designed to elicit the reaction it did.

Two variations on this theme offer similar responses. Either when the client does not understand something we just said or when we do not understand what the client said, we can act as though it is the client's fault. A stoney, quizzical face is quite effective in driving home the point that in close calls the therapist gets the benefit of the doubt. This implicit rule of thumb also allows us to sit silently when we do not know what to do next. The client may feel the responsibility to keep the ball rolling and say something emotional or intelligent.

Perhaps these games are necessary to increase the stature, omnipotence, and hence, influencing capabilities of the therapist—but it is always at the expense of genuineness, humanness, and presence that are so crucial in being with a client. People respond to us not only because of our professional competense but also because of our uniquely personal aura. The way we smile, laugh, love, give and the way our eyes twinkle teach clients as much about themselves as the most sophisticated interventions.

Counterfeit Intelligence. Another of several self-deceptions to be discussed is the most universal of therapist frauds. There we sit amongst our diplomas and memorabilia acting as if we knew exactly what we are doing. The collection of books and the wafting air of professionalism attest to our expertise. The client comes in self-possessed and off balance so what does he know? It takes the average client three to six sessions just to get his bearings, much less to decide whether this professional who comes so highly recommended is really a lightweight.

I can quote chapter and verse in Freud or any of the masters I have studied. I know exactly how to act like a therapist—that is, I have my penetrating stares, monosyllabic grunts, charming smile, and wise demeanor down pat. I know how to ask intelligent questions, to keep the conversation flowing, and every once in awhile, to say something fairly intelligent. If pressed, I can even tell a persistent client what I think his problem is and what he needs to do to make things better. Most of the time, if he follows my direction, he will get much better. But the truth of the matter is that throughout much of the encounter I am actually quite confused, uncertain, indecisive, and awkward. On the stage or in the therapist's chamber, the audience rarely discovers such lapses in performance.

A very prominent and successful psychoanalyst with twenty years of experience admits: "I tell myself because I've had so many years of experience I can handle whatever walks in the door. But I don't know if I will or I won't. I lie to myself and to my patients to feel the confidence I need to manage a professional practice. In truth I am extremely anxious every time I see a new patient. Will I understand him? Will I make an asshole of myself? Will I make a serious error in judgment? Will I know what to do? No. No. No. But I say to myself and to the client: 'Of course I can help you,' even when I think I can't."

Telling clients that we can help them is assuredly helpful even if it is not strictly true. Favorable expectations and placebo responses are set up principally by the therapist's belief in herself and the process. By communicating confidence, however false it might feel, we establish hope and motivation in the client. We would lose clients very quickly if after every bungled interpretation or misjudgment we muttered under our breath, but within earshot: "Oops. I blew that one." We would never get a client to come back if we were completely honest with them in the first sessions.

In other words, the client may need to believe in this lie and the others to be reviewed in order to get better. No physician in his right mind would ever let his uncertainties slip out, not just because he needs to protect himself from malpractice suits, but because people must have faith in their healers. Without faith there can be no magic.

Certain lies may therefore be necessary, if not therapeutic. If lying to a client, deliberately or unintentionally, is unethical since it promotes deceit and deception, perhaps it is just as unethical to be completely truthful (whether it is in the client's best interest or not) just so the therapist can feel pure. Tactical deception, then, has its place to protect clients from a reality they are not yet prepared to face or in the paradoxical interventions that break stubborn destructive patterns resistant to more conventional attacks. Although they are very effective strategies and quite useful in moving progress along, they are not usually one's first choice. No matter how we rationalize the necessity of the lie, whether exaggerating our powers or confidence, a certain amount of caution, modesty, and uncertainty is very helpful to keep us from getting too big for our own or the client's good. Just because we must tell the client that we know we can help him does not mean we have to believe it too. But it sure helps.

The Pretense of Perfectionism. Closely related to projecting a false sense of confidence is counterfeit expertise. This occurs when we pretend to know how to do something that we really do not know how to do.

- How many times have you said something you did not understand even if the client pretended he did?

- How many times have you hid behind a pregnant pause just to give yourself time to figure out where to go next?
- How many times have you heard a client say after a week of reflection: "I finally understood what you were doing last session and what it meant" and had no idea what profound insight you were supposedly developing?
- How many times has a referral contact or colleague or client asked you if you know how to work with a particular disorder, and you replied "Yes," while you scanned your bookshelves for a quick education?
- How often have you been asked by an inquisitive client what is going on and turned the question back to them until you could make something up?

The pretense of perfectionism may be for the client's benefit, but it affects the therapist as well. If we believed that we really were as thoroughly competent and composed as the image we present to clients, we would be insufferable to live with. Yet, if we were continuously honest with ourselves regarding what we know, what we understand, and what we can do, we would be so riddled with self-doubt we could barely function at all. The compromise position is to accept that we exaggerate our capabilities, that such distortion is sometimes necessary for the client's good, but that we should not for a minute forget that we are just pretending. "And if you pretend really well, the people you work with will pretend to make changes. And, they will forget that they are pretending . . . for the rest of their lives. But don't be fooled by it" (Milton Erickson quoted in Bandler and Grinder, 1979, p. 136).

Letting Go. Any time we act for reasons other than to promote the client's growth we dilute our honesty. This occurs occasionally, especially when we become more familiar with a client we have known for awhile. In addition to the effort we expend in taking care of clients, we take care of ourselves at the same time. This happens at the invitation of the client or sometimes by our own initiative.

Saying good-bye to a client is so bittersweet that many therapists encounter difficulty letting go. In most cases letting go represents a successful cure. The client has learned her lessons well, accomplished her goals, obliterated her suffering, and (hopefully) weaned herself of dependency on the therapist in the process. She feels strong, confident, insightful, and motivated to get on with the rest of her life. She also feels quite grateful to her helper, sad, nervous, and ambivalent about ending this relationship. The therapist shares many of the client's emotions: he feels excited, relieved, and probably confused as well.

Launching a client into the world leaves a vacancy in his schedule. It means a loss of revenue, a disruption in weekly routine that may have spanned years, and letting go of a dear and trusted friend. Even when it is in the best interest of the client to leave therapy, when the clinician claims to be doing everything in his power to help promote autonomy, his behavior may reveal quite different intentions. After all, keeping a client locked into treatment, with no hope or wish for escape, can ensure a therapist a lifetime income. It is inconvenient to replace a "good" client who knows the rules and does not demand very much for her money.

We all know practitioners who keep their clients addicted to them for decades. They teach people to need them, to require a weekly or daily fix just to function. Of course, some very disturbed people will need therapy throughout their lifetimes just to keep themselves out of the hospital. But here we are referring to those therapists who keep clients long beyond the point where they are doing them any good. One such psychiatrist has been seeing the same twenty clients two to four times per week for decades. His clients are so well heeled (and he is so reluctant to lose income) that when he schedules his annual vacation to the Caribbean he reserves the wing of a motel so that his clients may join him and continue their treatment. It is his opinion, and his clients readily and hysterically agree, that they just cannot function for two weeks without their doctor.

To a lesser extent any clinician in private practice struggles with the issue of when to let clients go. It is easy to say that as long as they keep coming to sessions they must be getting something from the experience. When working for a public agency, the longest I ever saw a client was for fifteen to twenty sessions. At the time I thought I was doing marvelous work. It can hardly be a coincidence that now that I am in private practice, where my very livelihood depends on my ability to keep my schedule full, the average number of sessions I see a client has jumped to forty. I have, naturally, convinced myself that this longer-term approach is much better for the client; it is more intense, more comprehensive, more elegant, more satisfying, more effective, and, yes, more costly.

A psychologist in private practice who is driven towards a goal of financial independence and yet also very dedicated to helping people admits with great discomfort: "I lie when I tell myself I can see thirteen clients in a day and not lose my effectiveness. I hypnotize myself into believing that so I can continue with this ferocious schedule I call my life. Especially I lie whenever I say that I am not doing this kind of work to make a lot of money. Because I am." This is certainly part of what motivates many therapists in private practice—not only to enjoy freedom but to strike it rich. And this attitude affects the pace and style of what we do.

Many things can be said about therapists—that we are knowledgeable, dedicated, compassionate—but we are rarely described as swift in our methods. We take our sweet time in getting to the heart of the matter, embellish our insights with poetry and stories, follow a tortuous route to a client's underlying fears. The lie to clients and to ourselves is that we will rid them of their symptoms just as fast as we can. Even a first-year intern knows that if you take away the client's presenting complaints too quickly, they will not stick around for the best part of the show.

Absolutes. A psychology professor reveals: "It's difficult to admit I lie. I can't really think of any ... well ... maybe there's one. I tell my students to have faith in the human capacity for healing. I talk about it as an absolute, but it isn't really. There's a lot of people I don't trust or who can't take care of themselves. Their instincts are all wrong."

There is a tremendous difference between our theories and our actual behavior. To the public, to clients, to colleagues we disclose our neat, coherent little models of why things work the way they do. Most practitioners, with little prodding, can articulate fairly detailed theories about human development, psychopathology, personality development, and psychotherapy. Together with these models of understanding, we also ascribe to specific systems of logic, morality, and epistemology. Finally, we bestow ourselves with titles to summarize the conceptual frameworks to which we owe allegiance: humanist, behaviorist, existentialist, Adlerian, Freudian, Reichian, eclectic. And therein hides the lie.

If the truth were told, most clinicians just do not apply their orthodox theories in their sessions—and for good reasons. Once a person, any person, applies a method invented by someone else it becomes a different method. Each therapist is simply too individual, with her distinct values, personality, demeanor, and voice, to ever practice therapy the same way another does. Moreover, the interactions with clients force one to think on one's feet, instantaneously, instinctually, no matter what training was received. If we were to stop and think, to reflect on our theories, we would interfere with the smooth flow of action as well as paralyze ourselves with complexity (Schön, 1983). In other words, we do not really function professionally like we say we do, or even like we think we do.

In spite of our labels as social worker or psychologist, counselor or psychiatrist, in spite of our identification with particular theories, we act in accordance with our intuition at the time. Most of the absolutes and rules that we say we follow are used only when appropriate or convenient. The most nondirective of practitioners occasionally gives advice. The most orthodox analyst reveals a distinctly human character. The most rigid rational-emotive therapist will also deal with feeling. And then there are the absolute imperatives of the profession that we all ignore at some time or another.

- *Do not give advice.* We do it all the time when a client is about to do something destructive.
- *Do not answer questions.* But we do answer them when we get tired of playing games or when we know the answer and are dying to tell someone.

- *Do not talk about yourself.* Although this may be desirable, it is idealistic and ultimately impossible.
- *Trust the client's capacity for healing.* If they had sound judgment concerning what is best for them, they would hardly end up in therapy.
- *Do not get involved in your client's life.* This is possible only if you sleep through the sessions.
- *You have to like your clients in order to help them.* But for a long time, some of them are genuinely unlikeable.
- *Refer those clients who are beyond your specialties and expertise.* If we did this, we would grow very little and have very few clients.
- *Personality disorders are genuinely untreatable.* But someone has to keep trying.
- *Let the client lead the sessions.* If the client cannot lead his life, how is he going to be in charge of his cure?
- *Protect the confidentiality of the client.* If you do not, you will be vulnerable to a lawsuit.

Myth of Neutrality. One of the foundations of our work is that we are professionals and experts who, like judges or arbitrators, are purported to be objective, detached, free of biases and prejudices, and morally neutral. Generations of therapists and clients have been deluded into believing in the myth of neutrality in helping—that it is not only desirable but possible to attain. We are cautioned to guard against exposing our true feelings, our prejudices, our convictions, and our values so we do not use undue influence, so we do not impose our morality on others. While those in pastoral counseling make no pretense of disguising their moral agenda, nonreligious practitioners also have a value program of their own. It may be to adopt a particular life-style, a way of thinking or feeling, a political orientation, or a preference toward particular ideas. But basically we want to sell our values of health, risk, honesty, emotional fitness, autonomy, and independence. These are considered "good" values, so they are exempted from the neutrality gag order. But "bad" values like dependence or safety should not be communicated, even if we may sometimes wonder if there is anything so terribly wrong with two people contentedly stuck in a fused, parasitic marriage. There is room for much philosophical debate here—and that is exactly the point. As therapists feel differently about love, marriage, commitment, sexuality, and relationships, so will they work differently in their sessions. Some clients really understand this, so they ignore our lies.

> The phone rings.
> "Do you do marriage counseling?"
> "Yes, I do."
> "Are you pro or against marriage?"
> "That depends on the marriage."
> "Let me put it differently. Do most of your couples stay together or get a divorce?"

Some perceptive clients are right on target with their queries. There are indeed therapists who stress commitment over divorce, sexual affairs over boredom, religion over education, travel over gardening, exercise over television, tea over coffee. We are hardly neutral, even if we try to keep our opinions to ourselves. We have opinions about everything a client says or does. And in the midst of our supposed posture of acceptance, unconditional positive regard, and neutrality, we are sometimes thinking to ourselves: "I wish you wouldn't."

London (1985) believes that, in spite of the myth, therapists are hardly value free, are rarely objective or neutral, and are, in fact, moral agents for their own beliefs. As human beings and members of society, therapists make a number of moral commitments. London points out that moral neutrality is itself a moral position that legitimizes the therapist's preference for freedom, democracy, independence, responsibility, and productivity.

A case could even be made that we ought to be even more forceful with our values and less morally neutral, or at least do away with much of the pretense. If a suicidal client enters our office, we will do our best to convince him to develop our respect for life. Should a client who lives by her wits, a gambler, a risk taker, a reckless sensation seeker wish our counsel, she will probably get a lecture on living more responsibly. We recommend the books that are most consistent with our life philosophy. In our hearts we believe that what is good for us is good for everyone. Therapists who enjoy traveling urge their clients to travel more. Those who find peace running on a country road or worshipping in a church would probably prefer to have their clients do the same.

If we choose not to impart any particular values, then we will push the big ones—that values are a good thing or that therapy is a marvelous experience that everyone should share. Other essential values espoused by most therapists are clearly articulated by Strupp (1980), Gross and Kahn (1983), Van Hoose and Kottler (1985). They found that clinicians ranked self-respect, friendships, personal pleasure, individual freedom, and universal love over social or religious institutions. We have a strong bias toward responsibility for our thoughts and action. We bristle at domination, coercion, manipulation. We think insight is a lovely thing, no matter what pain it will bring. In fact, we think pain is just fine too (especially when it is the psychic kind that belongs to someone else). Even within the client-centered camp there is a movement away from value neutrality. Boy and Pine (1982) suggest that therapists should become more explicit in communicating their values—especially those of free will and a definition of what is good and right.

If we do project our values during our work, what are the personal consequences for both client and therapist? We must shoulder the burden not only of relying on our clinical judgment and professional skills but of knowing clients will adopt many of our most personal beliefs. Are we really certain that the way we are living our lives is all that great for the rest of the world? We can justifiably worry whether it is in anyone else's best interest to adopt some of the values of a typical therapist. Some of our clients come in as just plain folks, naive and sheltered. They may leave enlightened, but at the expense of their innocence.

A Therapist's Personal Skills

The preceding sampling of absolutes that are not strictly followed only illustrates the discrepancy between what we say and what we do. These deceptions contribute further to the stress and confusion that therapists experience. Maybe it is our ultimate hypocrisy. While we push clients to expand their potential, strive for greater honesty, work to improve their personal effectiveness, we sometimes continue a life of mediocrity. In our offices we are stars—energetic, capable, creative, and powerful. Then we pack up our briefcases and head out into the world, fraudulent heroes.

There is often a major gap between the self our clients come to know and love and the self that we expose to the rest of the world. We are taught to keep our distance from students or clients during accidental social encounters—supposedly to protect them from embarrassment because we have such intimate knowledge of their lives. But another reason for this distance is to shelter them from the disappointment of finding out we are really quite human. We feel shy and inept. We are not as witty and wise outside our realm. We are threatened by strange situations just like everyone else.

Nevertheless, we are aware of the myth of personal competence we perpetuate. While a client complains of some self-defeating behavior or another, we smile condescendingly and ask: "So how can you live with yourself knowing you are impaired?" But how many times do we ask a client to master a skill we have not yet mastered or confront a problem that is still unresolved for us? One charismatic therapist reveals his most painful lie:

> There is great dissonance between what I ask my clients to do and what I am able to do in my own life. In relationships, for example, I encourage people to be less defensive in their communication and more empathetic with their spouse, while I'm aware in my own life I don't deliver on that stuff at all. There is a gigantic schism between my personal self and my much healthier professional self. I struggle to integrate the two parts of me. If I wasn't a therapist I would do just fine because I would be less in touch with the ideal self I want to be. But I *am* a therapist. I access my ideal self most

often when I'm working. I'm trying very hard to
do that more often when I'm outside my office.

A therapist is, beyond all else, a fully functioning model
for others to emulate, a personally and professionally masterful
human being (Vriend and Dyer, 1973; Kottler, 1983). What are
those idealized parts of ourselves we access during work hours
but are reluctant or unable to use otherwise? What are the skills
and insights we wield so masterfully with clients but somehow
forget during personal encounters? Many, many professional
skills do carry over to the personal realm. Most therapists, for
example, are quite astute at picking up on vulnerabilities of various people, filing them away, and using them to their advantage
at a later time. Therapists are also quite adept at using their
nondefensive confrontation skills or summarizing abilities during normal interactions. But then there are all those things we
know how to do, things we do every day, that we do not use as
much as we could to enrich the quality of our lives and of those
around us.

Focus. When we are receiving monetary compensation for
our time, we are more than willing to single-mindedly focus on
another person. Through our body posture, eye contact, and
other attending behaviors, we communicate our total interest in
whatever the client is saying. We hang on every word, note the
most subtle nuances of their nonverbal cues, sometimes even
take notes on the most inane details of their lives. We always
ask pertinent questions and further demonstrate our intense interest by frequently reflecting back to the client what we heard.
All of this is quite wonderful, so much so that a client feels appreciated and understood and is willing to pay lots of money
for the privilege.

A few hours later we are sitting at home talking to our
best friend on the phone while doing a crossword puzzle. We
absentmindedly listen to our loved ones, the people who we
prize above our own lives, while glancing through the newspaper, reviewing bills, or simply retreating inside ourselves. The
focused interest we are willing to sell we will not give away to
the people who matter most.

Compassion. No matter how bizarre or abusive a client

becomes, we usually turn the other cheek. With total concern and complete empathy we crawl inside someone else's sandals, boots, or Guccis and feel what they are feeling. Because we fully understand the pain they are experiencing we can be accepting and nondefensive in responding to their anguish. We can duck their anger and diffuse our own frustration in not striking back. A policeman sincerely responds, after just wiping the spit off his face from a burly felon he just arrested: "Look, if I've done anything to offend you, I apologize" (Ram Dass and Gorman, 1985, p. 45). The criminal apologizes as well, as people are prone to do when they are treated with compassion.

We feel self-satisfied after such a charitable gesture with a client. We reveal love instead of hate. Then we get in the car to drive home. Someone cuts us off on the freeway, someone with an ax to grind for who-knows-what reason. We scream obscenities at them, make rude gestures, and tailgate the offender for three minutes in retribution.

Respect. Unconditional regard and respect for the individual is something we practice effortlessly with a client. We genuinely believe in the intrinsic worth of an individual. We teach the philosophy of respecting other people's rights and dignity, at least during work. How much respect do we genuinely feel for and demonstrate toward the many people we encounter in the street? The wino singing in the alley, the man at the car wash who holds the door and waits for a tip, the kid who will guard your hubcaps for a buck? Gone are the focused interest, the compassion and regard, the respect for each person as a precious being.

Patience. For someone who can sit still in a chair hour after hour, a therapist sure has a hard time waiting in lines. Probably because we must wait so patiently during work we are reluctant to do so on our own time. Of all the qualities we must develop, patience is the most difficult: waiting for people to move at their own pace, waiting years sometimes before we can see a noticeable difference in a client's behavior.

Put this expert "waiter" in a room full of people and she will elbow her way to the front, if not to the center of attention, then to the head of the buffet line. A therapist discloses:

I really don't understand it. I am *so* patient in my therapy. I used to practice outwaiting a client during silences just to stay in shape. Now I think my greatest strength as a therapist is to allow my patients to take the time they need. I will sometimes push them, but only after they have taken the initiative. My interpretations are usually subtle and understated. I wait for clients to hear them when they are ready. . . . If not, (*shrugs*) we've got nothing but time. The really strange thing is that people always tell me I make them nervous because I'm always in a hurry. I'm the prototype of a Type A personality. I have only one speed outside of my office—blazing fast. On the phone I refuse to be on hold for more than thirty seconds. That's my rule. I'd rather hang up and do something else. I got in a bad habit checking my watch during sessions. I time myself going everywhere. People think I am the most impatient person alive. Only my patients know what I'm really like.

Spiritualism. Therapy sessions are packed full of lofty ideals; of mysticism; of higher consciousness; of ontological meaning; of transcendent states; of mind, matter, and oneness with the universe. Therapy works with the three "eyes of the soul": the "eye of flesh," which perceives the external world; the "eye of reason," which categorizes and analyzes data from the senses; and the "eye of contemplation," "by which we rise to a knowledge of transcendent realities" (Wilber, 1983, p. 3). The eye of contemplation is especially relevant to most therapeutic issues, for contained within it is all that is subjective, intuitive, spiritual. The therapist works with a "scope to human existence beyond egoism or personal power" (Hayward, 1984, p. 285). The client is taught not only about his thoughts and feelings and behaviors but about the softness of his heart and the spirit within him. Why, then, if we are so concerned about educating other people's spirits do we so neglect our own?

Historically, therapists were always poor. They were Buddhist monks, Socratic scholars, priests, wanderers, healers. What they lacked in material affluence they made up for in wisdom and purity of the soul. They felt that to be optimally clear, to understand the nature of all things, to enter someone else's soul, to take away pain, they would first have to leave behind their attachment to the material world. Only in the last century have therapists attained opulence in addition to (or instead of?) their spiritual power.

Many in the private sector gross six-figure incomes. And those in academia, in public and social service, in agencies and institutions, however meager their salaries, nevertheless stretch their money for all its worth. And now, after working so hard for the money we earn, we feel that we deserve to indulge and entertain ourselves. So our bodies are well fed and our minds are stimulated, but our spirits are undernourished, longing for the third eye of contemplation that gives meaning to existence.

Self-Control. The self-control of which therapists are capable is obvious. We ignore grumbling stomachs, the urge to yawn, and little voices whining: "Me, take care of *me.*" We restrain our impulses to hug, shake, kiss, or strike a client. We sit immobile for hours on end.

How then do we excuse our frequent lack of self-control at home? Gone is the willpower to refrain from overeating. Gone is the ease with which we can hold our temper. Gone is the resolve to stick with an exercise regimen. Where is the self-control that was so much in evidence just hours earlier? We plead exhaustion or a desire to escape from control. Time to relax in front of the television with a bowl of ice cream: "Will you kids shut up and give me some peace!"

There are many other things we do regularly while working that we do not do while on our own time. It probably could not be any other way. The lie is not in our inconsistency, not in our laziness and indulgences, but in our perpetuating the myth of our invulnerability. In many ways it is helpful for clients to hold on to this myth. It empowers our role as models. It keeps their attention and stimulates hope. But it is also very confusing for the therapist who must lead a double life, disguising a secret identity.

During a lengthy interview for this book, one therapist was startled by being asked about his lies and self-deceptions. After several minutes of thought he shrugged and said that he really could not think of any self-deceptions that he was aware of. He is a very honest person and, after years in treatment and supervision, feels very clear and self-aware. I turned off the tape recorder and began to pack up when I heard him clear his throat and whisper in a soft voice: "Everything I've said to you is a lie. It is so important to me to sound and look good that on some level I'm always suspect. I try my hardest and I still can't overcome my need to say and do things other people will approve of. I'm especially an imposter whenever I act like I know what I'm talking about. Even this is a lie."

EIGHT ✿✿

Alternative Therapies
for Therapists

Some of the problem areas therapists confront are the predictable result of prolonged practice; some are the result of self-deception and self-destructiveness. These are, of course, in addition to the "normal" crises that every human encounters: the usual variety of personal conflicts, insecurity, mood swings, restlessness, financial pressure, family problems, indecision, stagnation, fears of love, of death, of life. But, unlike the public at large, many therapists are well versed in the techniques of avoiding therapeutic experiences—whether these involve counseling ourselves or getting help elsewhere. Those therapists who do make personal growth a major life priority may, in fact, only go through the motions of a cure. For example, the most popular alternative for therapists who seek greater self-awareness and clarity is to undergo a form of psychoanalysis that is part of one's training. Unfortunately, by and large, therapists often make miserable clients. When it comes to changing our own behavior, we are perfectly skilled at pretense and acting.

A senior psychoanalyst admits: "My biggest lie to myself is when I say I've been psychoanalyzed. Even though I was in analysis for seven and a half years, I was a terrible patient. By no stretch of one's imagination could one say it was successful because I refused to allow several important areas of my life to be analyzed. Although I tell people all the time—clients, colleagues—that I've been analyzed, it's just not true. I've got a lot of work left to do."

Whether or not the therapist seeks enlightenment in the formal contexts of supervision, support groups, or psychotherapy, most practitioners are engaged, although not necessarily successfully, in counseling themselves. We just cannot talk to people all day long without hearing a little bit of what we say. We cannot teach people to talk to themselves differently without doing so ourselves.

The Therapist's Developmental Changes

As surely as we know any client will move through a progression of developmental stages throughout her life, or during the process of therapy, we know that we will experience a series of predictable, sequential, and logical changes during our professional careers. Most therapists begin their vocations from a position of idealism; a loss of innocence often follows. Next comes cynicism and a loss of enthusiasm followed, one hopes, by pragmatism coupled with realistic expectations, integrated experience, and greater flexibility.

Several critical incidents universally shape a therapist's development, the most obvious of which is the real reason the practitioner entered the field. Usually little similarity exists between the publicly espoused motives (some variation of the theme "to save the world") and those private, perhaps unconscious reasons (some variation of "to save ourselves"). We all have some hazy personal agenda we have been following since graduate school that responds to some internal force that pushed us into helping others and keeps us there. It could be to simulate the rescuer role that was familiar as a child, a way to get therapy for ourselves without having to risk the stigma of seeing a therapist. Becoming a therapist is one way some people seek to fulfill their need for power and control. Others are attracted to the opportunities for having successful relationships with minimum personal involvement. Still others who feel stupid can act wise, those who are selfish can pretend to be altruistic, and people who are timid can be assertive. One therapist relates: "If the truth be known, I could care less about the money and status. I don't spend much anyway. I don't even like working indoors, so it is hardly the comfort factor that keeps me seeing clients. But I do like people being dependent on me. I really do. I get off on being needed. Nobody ever needed me as a kid. I guess because I never had anything that anyone else ever wanted. Now I do. And people will drive long distances, pay money and jump through hoops for whatever it is I have. I like this feeling. No, I *love* this feeling."

What are the real reasons you became a therapist? Why do you really stay in the field when it is often much easier to try something else? What are you searching for in books such as this? The answers to these questions will provide the first clues to the critical incidents that shaped and continue to mold our development. These are precisely the areas that may have led us not only into the field but to our own therapy experiences as a client. These will continue to be the same issues we will always counsel ourselves about.

Previous experiences with therapy are often initial motivators to make the switch from client to helper. Many clinicians can trace their initial interest in the field, as well as their current style of practice, to the identification with a therapist who was instrumental in resolving some painful issues. There is a feeling of admiration for this powerful person who understands so much. There are feelings of gratitude and a wish to compensate for this guidance by passing it on to other generations. Since termination issues are never fully worked through, some clients become therapists so as to keep their own therapy going. A student relates: "My parents were so negligent that I was raised by therapists since I was fourteen. One after another they all tried to help me, to teach me. Some of them were pretty lousy—they would yell at me and tell me to grow up. Others were fantastic and immensely important. Here I am a grown woman who has been in therapy, on and off, for twenty-five years. I started training as a therapist because I couldn't find anyone left to work with. I figured it was about time I started helping myself— and maybe I could help some others in the process."

The problems that will require the most self-counseling during a therapist's life will be those that first appeared during the training years. Just as one's motives for entering the field and one's previous experience as a client set the parameters for what one will eventually become, one's graduate education and supervision will determine, to a large extent, the more specific forms of one's professional manner. During his apprenticeship, a student will undergo a radical transformation, only a small part of which will include the mastery of theories and skills; most of the changes involve a radical shift in one's thinking and one's self-concept.

During graduate education, the fledgling therapist is exposed to both positive and negative models. If she is unlucky she may even find herself caught in a political tug of war between two groups. For self-preservation she will identify with one group or the other. She will find sanctuary under the wing of a mentor and find solace in the books that speak to her. She will work hard to win the approval of her peers and instructors and, in so doing, will create a problem of external control she must counsel herself out of. For the rest of her life she may fight against the bondage created from years of working for grades. No matter how renowned she becomes she may yearn for the external approval she grew addicted to in her youth. She may look to her clients to find out how well she is doing, or measure her success by her income or schedule bookings. But forever she will wrestle with the need for affirmation. This is the gift from her instructors who taught her to depend on their grades, their evaluations, their commentary, and their approval to know how well she was doing.

Coupled with the need for external validation are the many internal changes a therapist will undergo. There is nothing like having one's hair turn grey, one's stomach turn finicky, or one's memory turn unreliable to facilitate a change in life philosophy, values, and therapeutic style. Spending day after day helping others deal with their failing health, decreased vitality, and developmental crises ought to make therapists better prepared to deal with their own. Yet in some ways it is worse, since the clinician must live through someone else's mid-life crisis a thousand times. We experience menopause and prostate problems, albeit vicariously, a hundred times. We live through the empty nest syndrome, launching adolescents, and meddling in-laws more times than we can count. By the time we must face these same problems we are already weary. We know what to expect and still cannot find ways to prevent those conflicts between parents and children that usually occur.

Fine (1980) describes a mid-life crisis that afflicts most therapists in the forty-five to fifty-five age bracket: the emergence of despair. This sadness of the soul originally explored by Chessick (1978) occurs as a result of a therapist's narcissistic vulnerability and prolonged exposure to sickness of the soul, "or, in more mythological terms, the petrification that results from gazing too far, too long, and too deeply at the psychotherapeutic Gorgon's head" (Fine, 1980, p. 393). There is, therefore, an accumulative erosion of will and depletion of spirit that culminates in the mid-life crises well-documented by Erikson (1963) and Levinson (1978). There are, of course, many other developmental crises therapists are hardly immune from.

We must counsel ourselves through those endless existential confrontations that "civilians" can easily hide from but therapists must face on a daily basis. When we hear clients confess they sometimes entertain fantasies of jumping off a balcony —just for the utter impulse of it—our knees feel weak the next time we look over a railing. Could I jump, too, just for the hell of it? We confront the big issues: death, the fear of going crazy, death, and death again. And always around the corner lies angst, nagging, tugging, tenaciously holding on. Angst is the dread that accompanies a life devoted to enlightenment. Without some form of therapy, it can infect the heart, mind, and spirit, leaving the victim in a state of permanent disillusionment.

Therapists' Resistance and Hypocrisy

For a group of people who spend their whole lives engaged in the practice of helping, we seem to exhibit a lot of resistance to getting it for ourselves. Several therapists who were interviewed for this book declined to comment on their self-deceit or their method of working through their own problems. Just before abruptly terminating the interview, one respondent typified the hostility and defensiveness this issue arouses:

"I don't ever lie to myself about anything, and I can't think of any way in which I might be self-deceptive. You ask me what I do when I encounter personal problems. One thing I would never do is see another therapist. I might try to work it through myself first, and then talk to my wife, but I would *never* go to anyone else. I just don't trust other professionals. And, even if I did, I've never had a reason to go."

Although this response is not typical of our profession, it occurred often enough to merit closer inspection. We may not all be as rigid, threatened, and mistrustful as this particular therapist, but many of us do seem to feel that therapy is for others. No less than a dozen therapists responded to the questions about personal problems and self-deception with a simple: "I can't think of any."

At first I wondered whether there might really be some among us who have attained a state of nirvana, perfect specimens of emotional and behavioral functioning who have transcended the problems of mortal beings. More than likely, questions that ask therapists to look at their vulnerabilities elicit the same kind of reactions as they would in a client. We deny we have problems. Those we grudgingly admit to, we think we can handle ourselves. We become defensive and irritable; we prefer our illusions of grandeur.

This resistance to examining ourselves with the same critical, diagnostic eye that we would direct toward a client amounts to utter hypocrisy. If we do not genuinely believe that the therapeutic tools of our profession can work on us, we have no business practicing them on anyone else.

Some Therapists Speak for Themselves

In addition to entering formal psychotherapy, there are a number of alternative methods that clinicians might use to pursue their own growth. A sampling of voices follows:

"My therapy is to do therapy. Being myself with my clients. I need a certain amount of contact with other people or I would stay alone. My clients affirm me, they challenge me, they push me to keep up with them."

"My therapy is talking with my wife. Sharing with her my fears. Opening myself up to her feedback. I think self-disclosure wherever and whenever I can is therapeutic for me. Telling people when I'm afraid. Forcing myself to be honest about what I'm feeling."

"I travel a lot as a way to energize myself. When I'm away on a trip I don't even think about my children, much less my clients. I don't know how I do it, but I do. Once I'm on the way to the airport I let go of everything. The geographic distance creates a psychological distance. I shed my skin as a therapist and become a person in movement."

"I'm so damn driven and ambitious I had to find a way to slow myself down. I needed to do something just for myself—not for an audience, not for my resume, not even for a sense of accomplishment. That's why I've been playing the guitar for two years and nobody has ever heard me. When I concentrate on the music I can't possibly think about anything else. For a few minutes nothing exists except my breathing, my fingers, the sounds I hear and feel."

"It started out that running was to be my therapy. It helped me sleep at night, forget my troubles, and do something nice for myself. Then I became obsessed and the cure became the problem. I developed knee and hip problems while training for marathons. After awhile I approached running like I do everything else: I became competitive and regimented. It was no longer an escape, but another obligation. Now I'm down to just a few miles a day and it helps a lot to keep myself centered."

"My therapy is gardening and digging in the dirt and watching things grow. My therapy is playing golf. My therapy is doing crossword puzzles. My therapy is being with friends, entertaining, going out. And sometimes, my therapy is just doing nothing, just nothing at all."

"Being a therapist helps me to question myself a lot, to ask myself what I need. When I can feel a knot inside me, I know it's time to go work out or just get under the covers for awhile.

"My husband is a wonderful help to me. He is very sensitive to me. He can sense what I need even before I do. He knows when I want to be hugged or when I want to be taken care of. I've been taking care of people all day long so when I get home I need time to let go."

"I live by certain rules. I never see more than eight clients in a day. I try not to see two appointments back to back. I spread them out over the week and leave deliberate holes during the middle of the day to feed myself, replenish myself. I read, go for walks, talk to friends during breaks. My therapy is in just the way I schedule myself so I don't feel overburdened."

These samples of therapeutic alternatives set the tone for what is possible in self-nourishment for professional helpers. Each of the self-administered therapies that will be reviewed are further examples of what clinicians often do to keep themselves emotionally fit and spiritually energized.

Self-Therapy

When Therapists Talk to Themselves. There are many
ways a therapist works to counteract angst and manage the
transformations that are part of the helping life-style. Talking
to ourselves as we would to clients is the most direct and effective cure. This self-administered therapy is especially advan-
tageous in those situations in which we may be needlessly
worrying about clients or having difficulty separating ourselves
from others. If we find, during odd moments of the day or
while tossing in bed, that we are unable to let go of our work,
we may initiate a self-dialogue such as the following: "How am
I helping my clients by spending time worrying about their
welfare? If I'm not helping them, then what is this behavior
doing for me? Inflating my sense of importance? Using magi-
cal thinking to prevent tragedy by anticipating it? Distracting
myself from something in me?"

Consistent with but not restricted to the tenets of
rational-emotive or cognitive-behavioral therapy is the suggestion that therapists use self-talk to dispute their irrational striv-
ings for success and perfection (Ellis, 1984). On a broader
scale, those confrontations, interpretations, and challenges that
produce the most dramatic impact on a client's behavior will
do the same for us. After all, we are experts at talking people
out of their suffering. We give pep talks that motivate clients to
overcome their fears. We convincingly challenge them to let
go of beliefs that are not helpful. We teach clients to talk to
themselves so that they may carry our voices with them wherever they may go. At times when they balk or stutter, our
words of encouragement come back to them. We repeat our
favorite strategies of self-talk so often they have become our
personal prayers. During moments of stress or difficulty, they
return to haunt us. There is nothing as uncomfortable for a
therapist as catching himself feeling self-pity and hearing his
own words in his mind, echoing exactly what he would say to
a client in a similar situation.

In fact, it is through the testing of a particular intervention on ourselves that we first discover its possible utility in

a session. A therapist who is gnashing his teeth in frustration over a difficult client notices he calms down considerably when he reminds himself: "This is what I'm paid for." The self-talk not only helps him to calm down, but later, with the same client, he is able to urge the use of this identical strategy: "You get so angry at the customers for complaining about their purchases, so instead you transfer your hostility to me. But what do you expect to hear while working in public relations? Customers are supposed to yell at you. So every time you let their whining get to you, just remember: Their job is to complain, yours is to listen without feeling defensive."

We are constantly telling people how to talk to themselves. An adolescent mourning the loss of his girlfriend is instructed to tell himself his pain is necessary and a sign of how much love he is capable of feeling. A woman straddling the line just this side of panic is urged to tell herself the impending attacks will subside if she will remind herself of where she is and what is really happening around her. An obese man is cautioned that every time he reaches for food he does not need he should tell himself he is hiding from his pain. By teaching others to counsel themselves at will, the therapist internalizes the same therapeutic messages.

We may find it necessary to counsel ourselves in the same situations in which we recommend that clients use self-talk.

- When we feel uncomfortable in social situations ("What have I really got to lose by approaching these people?")
- When the car will not start ("Getting mad right now is *not* going to start the car.")
- When we are about to lose our temper ("This just isn't all that important.")
- When we do not get what we want ("Oh well.")
- When we are about to do something that might get us in a lot of trouble ("Is it worth it, and if so, am I willing to pay the price of getting caught?")

There are also a number of instances in which the use of self-talk strategies are particularly helpful in a therapist's life:

- When a client becomes worse after our intervention ("I guess this means I'm not perfect and the client isn't yet ready to change. Time to try Plan B.")
- When one's mind drifts elsewhere during a session ("Concentrate. Concentrate.")
- When a client will not talk during a session ("Just relax. Take a deep breath. He'll talk when he has something to say.")
- When a client fails to show up for an appointment ("Don't take it personally. Getting mad isn't going to help the client and it surely isn't going to help me. What can I do with my time instead?")
- When a session is interrupted by someone knocking at the door ("No big deal. Let me just deal with this and then get back to work.")
- When a client does not pay his bill ("What an annoyance. How can I take care of this so that I won't have to think about it anymore?")
- When there is not enough work to do ("I guess it's time to hustle up some work. Things are always slow this time of year.")
- When there is too much work to do ("The world isn't going to end just because I don't finish all of this stuff today.")
- When a client becomes abusive ("Oops. I'm letting him get to me.")
- When we feel blocked with a client ("What is getting in the way of my being helpful?")
- When in spite of our best efforts the client does not improve ("I can't reach everybody all of the time.")

When we listen to our own interventions, apply them to ourselves during self-dialogues, we demonstrate the true effectiveness of what we teach. After having said these things to ourselves and noted the results, we have greater conviction in what we say to clients. Again we note the interaction between the personal and professional in a therapist's life. As we stumble across some way of expressing a motivational or insightful idea during a session, we rub our hands in glee knowing we can use it again and again with other clients and especially with ourselves. And when we encounter a particularly poetic expression during social conversations, while watching a movie, or while walking in the woods, we smile inwardly and store it away for later use.

When Therapists Solve Their Own Problems. A second set of strategies for therapist self-counseling involves treating ourselves as we would our clients by using our capacity for healing, nourishment, insight, and motivation to enrich our lives. This can range from simply noting our defensiveness in a threatening situation to designing an elaborate problem-solving package including short- and long-term goals, contingencies, reinforcements, and action strategies. By applying our therapeutic wisdom and skills to ourselves, we increase our personal effectiveness as we field-test our best interventions on our most severe critic.

Those practitioners who are behaviorally inclined have an incredibly wide range of techniques at their disposal to help in defining and solving problems. Even those therapists who work primarily with insight and deplore systematic training in decision making are nevertheless quite skilled at helping people get to the bottom of what is bothering them and then remedy the situation. Whether we teach problem-solving skills directly or by combining them with other interventions, we are experts at understanding how and why problems develop and what can be done to solve them, or at least live with them.

One psychologist feels especially successful at being his own best client when it comes to applying his problem-solving system to himself: "I am constantly applying the model that I use with my clients to myself. I try to define the problem I'm experiencing in specific operational terms. I look at the precipitating and contributing factors, the intervening variables, and why the problem continues to exist. I create a plan based on what I want and what needs to be done."

No other professional in any field works so intimately with the process of constructive thinking. As applied philosophers, we not only understand the intricacies of logic, ethics, metaphysics, and epistemology, but we are readily able to em-

ploy their methodologies in solving everyday problems. We
teach people how to think more rationally, to feel more appro-
priately, to behave more constructively. We can sort out the
complexities of that chaos we call emotional disturbance. We
know how to simplify the salient issues, shelve the distractions,
and focus in on the core issues. We are experts at ranking priorities in terms of their pertinence to desired goals. We can juggle
the different loose ends while we determinedly push forward
with a plan of action, then return to any number of related
themes that were left hanging.

We are not only masters of deductive and inductive reasoning, practical philosophers who can cut through the gristle to
the real meat of an issue but scientists by training and inclination. We use empirical methodologies to objectively evaluate the
effects of any variable or intervention. We test hypotheses in
our sessions with deceptive precision. We systematically collect
the data that are pertinent to a particular case, isolate the dependent variables, and then, with flexibility and stubbornness,
try out any number of treatment variables while scrutinizing
their impact on the client, on ourselves, on the flow and movement of the sessions.

That we can integrate so many skills and diverse bodies
of knowledge into a coherent system of problem solving is a
testimony to our potential for an ideally healthful existence.
The hard part is applying all that we can do to help clients
solve their problems to the resolution of our own. Even with
our defenses and subjectivity, with the limitations involved in
using oneself as an object of self-study, we can certainly accomplish more than we presently do.

The voice of a social worker: "I was stuck in my job and
couldn't see a way out. I had talked to a friend, even tried therapy myself for awhile, but nothing much changed except that I
developed even stronger excuses and better rationalizations for
avoiding change. Sometimes I hate being a therapist for just that
reason. Why can't I be more innocent and trusting—just let
things happen instead of analyzing everything? Anyway, for a
long time I gave up. I thought I had tried everything I knew
how, but I was a failure as my own client—or anyone else's for

that matter. But then I just let go. I'd done that before lots of times with clients. When they fight back or become defensive, I just let go. I tell them to keep their misery if they like it so much; they're just not ready yet to change. When I told a client that again for the fortieth time last month it occurred to me I could do that with myself, too. I did. And that's how I ended up in my new job."

Journal Keeping. A number of painfully introspective writers, including Anais Nin, John Steinbeck, Thomas Wolfe, Andre Gide, and Albert Camus, kept journals throughout their lives as a way to maintain their sanity and clarity after pouring out so much of themselves in their work. Carl Jung was the first to recognize the merits of the diary for a practicing therapist. It was in his Black Book that he first developed his theories; analyzed his dreams, fantasies, and symbols; recorded the events of his life; and conducted imaginary dialogues with his unconscious. Rainer (1978) found Jung's example inspirational, particularly when merged with the creative self-therapy approach of Anais Nin who devoted her life to exploring psychological themes as a woman, a therapist, and a writer. Jung opened a door that other clinicians were able to widen even further.

> Although Jung used the journal as a vehicle for a heroic journey into the sea of the unconscious, he concluded that an awareness of dreams and inner images always needs to be integrated with the pragmatic realities of everyday existence: "Particularly at this time, when I was working on the fantasies, I needed a point of support in 'this world.' It was most essential for me to have a normal life in the real world as a counterpoise to the strange inner world" [Jung quoted in Rainer, 1978, p. 22].

Writing letters to colleagues and friends can also be a form of self-therapy and catharsis for the therapist struggling with new ideas and insights or with his personal pain. Freud began his five-year correspondence with his best friend Wilhelm Fliess to explore his burgeoning theories and to promote his self-analysis. He did the same with trusted colleagues such as Jung. These early pioneers quickly discovered that in the role of confidant to others a structure must be created for the therapist to become a confidant to himself. Systematic journal writing serves just that function for therapists in several different ways (Dyer and Vriend, 1977; Kottler, 1983).

1. *It is a way to supervise oneself and work through difficulties with particular cases.* It could be said that all client resistance results, in part, from some blocking that occurs in the therapist. The journal provides a vehicle to explore the dynamics of being stuck with a client. We can examine our feelings and thoughts as they are elicited by a session's content. We can keep track systematically of the interventions we use with clients in given situations and note their specific effects. We can also outline in writing the facts and impressions of a case so as to structure alternative treatment plans.

The journal is useful for a therapist in following the patterns of his professional behavior over time. When we encounter a client with concerns similar to those we have resolved successfully or unsuccessfully before, we can review the interventions we tried before to avoid repeating mistakes. Naturally, journal writing is the single most helpful structure for working through feelings of countertransference with clients.

2. *It is a method of self-analysis.* Freud's need to pour out his feelings accelerated during the period of his greatest introspection: "My own analysis is going on, and it remains my chief interest. Everything is still dark, including even the nature of the problems, but at the same time I have a reassuring feeling that one only has to put one's hand in one's own store-cupboard to be able to extract—in its own good time—what one needs" (Freud, [1897] 1954, p. 227).

To extract what one needs becomes a much simpler task if there is some repository where things are stored. The journal becomes for the therapist a place to pour out his heart. It is the place for exploring one's hidden motives, unconscious desires, and unresolved struggles. It is the place for catharsis and free association, where dreams are expressed and analyzed, where the structure and patterns of one's life become evident.

3. *It is a vehicle for developing and recording ideas.* Many novelists have used their journals to create intricate plots, sketch their characters, or record ideas they may some day use. In his journal, Thomas Wolfe processed the work of his predecessors and scrupulously considered his contemporaries, attempting to define for himself the nucleus of all he would later write about: "Literature is, in any sense, a criticism of life. That criticism is either actual or implied. Especially does this hold true of drama. If we really desire literature, the artist must be given full scope in which to exercise his talent. . . . Any attempt to make him the creature of public squeamishness will kill him and his art. If we are not willing to meet these conditions, we are not ready for the art; we are not worthy of literature" (Wolfe, [1921] 1970, p. 7).

All therapists are theoreticians. We harbor our own unique ideas about how the world works and how therapy ought to be conducted. No matter what school of thought we align ourselves with, we have our own individual notions about how best to work. The journal is the best place to articulate these ideas, to formulate our theories, and to grow as thinking beings.

4. *It is a record of significant events.* Therapists are more aware than most of the value in studying one's past in order to make sense of the present and future. By reviewing the history of a client's developmental growth and studying the critical incidents in a client's life, we come to discover what is creating the present complaint. Our journal allows us to do this for ourselves.

There are milestones in anyone's life worth recording: births, deaths, job changes, the loss of innocence, successes, and failures. Journal keeping helps us maintain our perspective on where we have been and where we are going. It is a way to remember things we have experienced. And best of all, it becomes a structure for committing ourselves to future goals. As we work toward these goals, and counsel ourselves in the process, we become even more personally and professionally effective.

Exercise. Because we do our work sitting in a chair, using our intellect and voice, many therapists find relief exercising the body. While the mind remains active through its diagnostic and reasoning chores, the body remains inert, wasting away in some places and growing in others through neglect.

That therapists have jumped on the physical exercise bandwagon is not surprising. We who understand that total wellness requires the interaction of mind and body, who observe at close range how a sick brain can destroy a healthy body and how failing health can sap one's will feel committed to the nourishment of our total being. Whether the activity is intended primarily for aerobic conditioning, esthetics, entertainment, rehabilitation, or distraction, a regular exercise program serves a therapist's needs. The reasons for beginning such a program can be as varied as those for the population at large:

- to prolong life
- to increase self-discipline
- to serve as a self-medication for stress
- to improve esteem and confidence
- to make oneself more attractive
- for body cathexsis
- to sleep better
- to control weight

But therapists have other reasons to exercise: to engage in something nonverbal, to give oneself silent time in an enlightened state—time for processing the day, for calming down, for beginning or ending a day of confronting other people's troubles.

When I ride my bike the wind washes me clean. Everything I have soaked in during the previous days oozes out through my pores, all the complaints and pain and pressure. I feel only the pain in my legs and lungs as I climb up a hill pumping furiously. And then I coast down as fast as I can, never knowing what is around the next turn. For an hour or two I am no longer a receptacle for other people to dump their suffering. Nobody catches me on my bike. There is no chance to think or I will miss a pothole in the road. And it takes too much concentration watching for traffic, pacing my rhythm, switching gears, working on technique, saving my strength, breathing slow to consider anything outside my body. After a ride through the country, I feel ready again to face my clients, my past, and my uncertain future.

Group Support

In addition to attempting some form of self-therapy to promote serenity and enlightenment, a number of changes can be initiated to make life easier yet more stimulating. Maslach (1982), for example, suggests the use of group ritual for therapist nourishment. If certain rules can be imposed to severely curtail endless complaints or criticism (such as what occurs in many teachers' lounges), informal groups can provide a special source of energy. Moss (1981) finds the group to be a tremendous healing force for therapists in that there is a sense of sharing and of community, the embracing of relationships, and a universal, dynamic, and focused energy that everyone may draw inside their being. This is, of course, in addition to the usual transformational powers of a group through the dynamics of cohesion and intimacy. Moss feels certain key elements should be part of such a transformational group: several multidimensionally awakened people; a setting that is conducive to an inspired process; commitment on the part of participants to release old patterns, to trust, and to be together; the infusion of love; and grace.

Such support groups, in some shape or form, spring up spontaneously in organizations. A room, a tree, or a bench may be designated as an informal gathering place where clinicians can meet during breaks or between sessions. This sanctuary is a place to get a back rub or to talk about cases. It is a safe place to unload and release the negative energy that has accumulated during previous sessions. Therapists who work in isolation often organize a weekly meeting of minds and hearts outside of their offices.

Friendships and family supply a comparable source of support for many therapists. We all need a place we can go to

cleanse ourselves, to talk through our concerns, and keep our
mental and emotional functioning tuned up.

Even with regular therapy and supervision, a clinician still
needs daily support. This is often accomplished through debrief-
ings with one's spouse at the end of a day, with a special friend,
or with colleagues. As one clinician reports: "Even when I was
seeing a therapist once a week and paying for supervision twice
a week I still felt the need for something else. Talking to my
wife every night and a psychiatrist friend occasionally also took
some pressure off. But not enough. That's when I started roping
some colleagues to join me for informal gatherings during the
day. Whereas previously we would bitch together a lot—about
the paperwork, Blue Cross, or some departed associate—I began
asking them for help. Pretty soon we were all focused on the
problems we were having and what we could do about them. It
became not so much a therapy group as a bunch of people who
were open to whatever happened."

Adventure and Escape

One final form of therapy many practitioners choose to
reinvigorate themselves is vicarious or actual adventure. Camp-
ing out in front of the television for an evening or losing oneself
in a two-hour movie is a wonderful way to turn off one's brain,
sit passively, and allow other people to provide the entertainment. Escape fiction is an even better option since books take
longer to get through and the "treatment" can be self-administered as needed. I would expect that John D. MacDonald, El-
more Leonard, Robert Parker, Lawrence Sanders, and Robert
Ludlum have rescued more than one therapist from boredom
or despair.

Many enjoy more active forms of adventure and escape in
travel. Away from the office, our homes, our clients, and our
colleagues, we regain a perspective on what is important. There
comes a time when we grow tired of living out of a suitcase and
feel ready, if not eager, to return to that which we call work.

Any of the alternative therapies covered in this chapter
or any of the other creative endeavors in the one that follows

can serve as a means of escape, of detachment from the therapist's role. Our reservoir of energy is slowly depleted with every session we conduct until replenishment becomes a necessity rather than a choice. Whether the individual practitioner finds peace in a church or synagogue, in a theater, in a garden, in a sports arena, or on the road is beside the point. The important thing is to do something for ourselves so that we can take things less personally, lower our expectations to realistic levels, break away as we need it, and talk to ourselves as we do to our clients. Most of all, by doing something for ourselves, we demonstrate that we take our own growth just as seriously as we do the growth of those who buy our services.

NINE ✿✿

Toward Creativity
and Personal Growth

Everything comes together for a therapist in the creative process. Boredom, burnout, and other professional hazards are neutralized when we experience a major insight. Through an innovative procedure, we share our passion for discovery with the client.

The creative journey toward a new understanding, for the client or the therapist, follows a progression from the familiar to the unknown. During this passage there is a move from stable ground to confusion, frustration, self-doubt. To be successful in creative endeavors requires abandoning the verbal and the concrete for the uncertainties of intuition and subjectivity. Yet, despite the risks implicit in any creative endeavor, a therapist has little choice but to continue the natural evolution toward personal and professional growth.

The Urge to Create

Therapists are, at least theoretically, self-actualizing people. Maslow (1968) eloquently connected this intrinsic growth motive with the urge to create. He described one of his subjects, a psychiatrist and pure clinician who had little use for research or theory, as follows: "This man approached each patient as if he were the only one in the world, without jargon, expectations, or presuppositions, with innocence and naivete and yet with great wisdom, in a Taoistic fashion. Each patient was a unique human being and therefore a completely new problem to be understood and solved in a completely novel way" (p. 136).

Personal growth and creativity are synonymous in the life of a therapist. Ideally it is possible to use our creative thinking for the benefit of enlightenment. We do this in our offices as well as at home. A child therapist works in a solo practice but never feels lonely or isolated; instead she finds the solitude more conducive to trying things her own way: "At first I thought I don't really do much that is creative. I mean I don't write or anything like that. But I do many things that are indeed unusual. The way I do therapy always changes. I use art or music or movement or anything that strikes me at the time in my sessions. I trust that aspect of myself. I think the way that I live is creative. I have a great sense of humor. I *do* a lot of creative things. There are times I've awoken the kids at 2 A.M. to drive downtown for ice cream. Or sometimes I like to do crazy things like hide from my husband when he comes home from work and then jump out to scare him."

The creative urge in therapists is ignited not only by the challenge of a client's problem but by a person who "looks on the world as fit for change and on himself as an instrument for change" (Bronowski, 1978, p. 123). Much of our existence is defined by the ways we can leave the world different after we are gone.

Why do we experience the urge to create, if not "to reach beyond our own death" (May, 1975, p. 17)? On the simplest level, the most basic of all human drives is to create another life in our own image, to perpetuate our gene pool. Our very survival as a species has not only depended on the persistence of our progeny, but on our ability as versatile, cunning, and creative problem solvers (Breuer, 1982).

Therapists have more than their share of creative energy. Our ideas live for generations through every client we help. People may forget their grocer or their fourth-grade teacher or neighbor, but they never forget their therapist. What a client will remember about his therapist is likely to be a particularly novel idea she introduced to him or a familiar concept that was presented in an instructive way. For this reason, a therapist will live as long as her ideas survive.

Resistance to Creativity

On first sight, creative acts are often viewed as a form of deviance. A brief glimpse into our field's history reveals a number of contributions that were initially scorned and ridiculed. Neither Freud nor anyone who has come on the scene since has had an easy time finding a sympathetic audience for his radical approaches to helping.

People are threatened by new ideas that challenge what they think they already know. Resistance to creative thinking is much more the norm than the exception. Especially in the evolution of science, professional thinkers have much preferred esthetics and symmetry in their ideas than the chaos of reality. Boorstein (1983, p. 86) comments on why it took so long for explorers, who long had the necessary technology, to find and plot the geographical world: "The great obstacle to discovering the shape of the earth, the continents, and the ocean was not ignorance but the illusion of knowledge. Imagination drew in bold strokes, instantly serving hopes and fears, while knowledge advanced by slow increments and contradictory witnesses. Villagers who themselves feared to ascend the mountaintops located their departed ones on the impenetrable heavenly heights."

One scientist who sought to climb the mountain and find out for himself why so many people depart life before their time was Ignay Semmelweiss. Koestler (1964) mentions his case as an example of the inevitable and stubborn resistance that accompanies any creative act that revolutionizes our thinking. In 1847 Semmelweiss discovered that it was the filth, bacteria, and residual cadaveric material on a surgeon's hands that caused infections in patients who became worse after operations. "As an assistant at the General Hospital in Vienna, Semmelweiss introduced the strict rule of washing hands in chlorinated lime water before entering the ward. Before this innovation, one out of every eight women in the ward had died of puerperal fever; immediately afterwards mortality fell to one in thirty, and the next year to one in a hundred. Semmelweiss's reward was to be hounded out of Vienna by the medical profession—which was moved, apart from stupidity, by resentment of the suggestion that they might be carrying death on their hands. He went to Budapest but made little headway with his doctrine, denounced his opponents as murderers, became raving mad, was put into a restraining jacket, and died in a mental hospital" (pp. 239-240).

A similar but less dramatic fate of ostracism befell many other creative geniuses—Copernicus, Galileo, Darwin, Mozart, Van Gogh—to name but a few representatives of their fields. In most cases a creative idea is first viewed with suspicion and resentment. Perhaps this probationary period is constructive in that it filters out many worthless eccentricities; those that can stand the test of time and the criticism of their peers endure.

For pioneering therapists creativity is often resisted because it usually involves breaking rules. Our culture may endorse the idea of creativity, but it certainly does not embrace new structures that make the old ones obsolete. Within our field Bloom (1975) mentions how creative acts often stand in opposition to the structures that were built by those currently in power. Inevitably there will be tension and conflict before the new ideas can be accepted. When breaking rules for the sake of finding successful, novel solutions to client problems Bloom suggests remembering the following points:

1. All rules will eventually be broken.
2. Be prepared to face the consequences (tension and wrath) after introducing a new idea.
3. Compare the effectiveness of old and new before making a public pronouncement.
4. Assume that every client deserves to be treated as a unique and individual challenge that deserves a creative solution.
5. Not all creative ideas are good ideas. Some are not practical, some are not useful, others are downright dangerous in that they could harm more people than they could ever help.
6. Creativity involves taking risks.

Risking and Creativity

Risk and fear are synonymous. There cannot be the possibility of gain without the possibility of loss—no matter how carefully one anticipates and prepares. Taking risks means, to some, the possibility of making the wrong choice. In almost all cases it means breaking the rule of the status quo.

Creative acts are risky because they deal with unknown consequences. For this very reason the tightrope walker Philipe Petit, who danced on a cable suspended between the two tallest buildings in the world, laughed at being called a risk taker: "I have no room in my life for risk. You can't be both a risk taker and a wirewalker. I take absolutely no risks. I plan everything the most that I can. I put together with the utmost care that part of my life" (Keyes, 1985, p. 10).

The risk in trying something new in therapy is that it is possible, if not probable, that it will not work in the first several attempts. We risk losing our way and becoming lost.

The process of doing therapy awakens in us the sense of ourselves as explorers. We teach others to discover unchartered territory, to learn survival skills and apply them in conditions of maximum stress. We teach people about their limits and their capabilities. We help people take controlled risks where much of the danger can be anticipated.

Yet failure and some risk cannot be avoided if the possibility of success is to have any meaning. There are risks of emotion that involve honestly and spontaneously expressing feelings, admitting fear, or professing love. There are risks of growth in giving up control, in being yourself, or in trying something that has never been attempted before. There are risks of intimacy in working through vulnerability, jealousy, and trust. There are risks of autonomy in cutting off dependencies and being more responsible. And there are risks of change that involve breaking old rules, patterns, and habits and moving into the world of the unknown (Viscott, 1977).

Creative Problem Solving

Some of the best examples of creative problem solving come from the family therapy practitioners who seek to break rigid hierarchies of power and vicious cycles designed to repel any outside intervention. Innovation and experimentation are the hallmarks of these strategic helpers who rely on strange, novel, sometimes hilarious means to initiate change in difficult clients. In describing the methodologies of famed healer Milton Erickson, Haley (1973) recited a litany of radical and seemingly ridiculous cures that involved prescribing the symptoms, encouraging resistance or a relapse, or telling apparently distracting stories. Haley (1984) developed even further the concept of creative problem solving in his own brand of ordeal therapy, which seeks unusual ways of changing behavior by presenting an alternative to the client that is even less desirable than his symptoms. In this form of helping, the therapist is encouraged to think outside the usual parameters of our field. The lesson in this is certainly not that we should all be practicing this often bizarre form of treatment with its own problems in downplaying the client's responsibility in the process, minimizing the value of insight, and deliberately perpetuating more mystery and manipulation than is probably needed. Rather, family and strategic therapists offer encouragement to (1) be flexible and maneuverable in the ways we position ourselves in relation to the client (Fisch, Weakland, and Segal, 1982); (2) be playful, spontaneous, dramatic, and intuitive during sessions (Satir and Baldwin, 1983); (3) use whatever the client presents in his symptoms, behavior, or resistance as the leverage to initiate change (Erickson, 1964); (4) when you try something that fails to work, try something, anything else (Bandler and Grinder, 1979); (5) free yourself of the constraints of needing to be correct and give yourself permission to be ineffective for long enough until you can find something that does work (Minuchin and Fishman, 1981); (6) do what feels right at the time (Napier and Whitaker, 1978); (7) understand client symptoms as creative solutions to their problems (Madanes, 1981); (8) appreciate the absurdity of human dilemmas and the paradox of life, treating symptoms in a similar context (Haley, 1984).

When these cries for intuition and creativity are combined with our natural heritage of empiricism, philosophical inquiry, and the rigorous applications of scientific methodology, we have at our disposal a process that is both creative and cautious, radical and responsible. Clients come to us only after they have already exhausted the more traditional and obvious problem-solving strategies. They have discovered that drugs do not work for very long. Nor does blaming others or wishing that problems would magically vanish. Hiding under the covers feels safe until you have to change the sheets. Faced with nowhere else to go, all other options eliminated, they walk into the therapist's office defeated. Obviously the cure will be found in something the client has not yet tried, or in the case of very difficult clients, in what no other physician or therapist has yet discovered.

Creative Thinking

In an essay for researchers on breaking out of their conceptual ruts and away from the tendency to think as clones of one another, Wicker (1985) offers some advice that may be applied with equal usefulness to the fostering of creativity in therapists:

1. A playful, whimsical attitude can be adopted by exploring unusual metaphors.
2. A therapist should constantly tinker with the assumptions of her operating principles, especially those she holds most sacred.
3. She should also attempt to expose hidden assumptions by increasing awareness of implicit processes in her work.

The therapist functions much of the time as a detective. First, we attempt to figure out the crime a client feels he has committed that is bad enough to warrant symptomatic punishment. We interview the suspect, reconstruct the crime, and carefully gather evidence. We formulate a motive, a hypothesis regarding how and why the symptoms appeared. We deduce a modus operandi, a signature to the crime, a pattern in which the current symptoms fit the client's characteristic style. We gently interrogate the client, squeeze out a confession that will exhaust the need for continued self-punishment. In these activities it is the therapist's willingness to enter the client's world, to sift through all the information available, and, finally, to connect events and intuitively interpret their meaning that will solve the problem. To accomplish these tasks, the therapist must be a creative detective, must be able to see beyond the obvious, to the often disguised and subtle clues that lie embedded in a client's behavior.

Doing Therapy as a Creative Enterprise

There are essentially two points of view in practicing therapy. One approach emphasizes reliability and consistency in interventions. To minimize chance variables and maximize intentionality, Kagan (1973) feels it is crucial for therapists to be able to replicate what they do. When you find something that works—a particular anecdote or metaphor, a structure or intervention, an interpretation or technique—you should, according to this approach, use it again and again. To not do so is to cheat the client of a well-tested remedy that is known to be effective.

For example, one standard and reliable response to the client complaint "I'm not getting any better" is "Then the therapy must be working since it is helping you to become uncomfortable and therefore more motivated to change." It is not that relying on this well-worn intervention does not work, because it is consistently effective, but rather that the therapist begins to feel like a computer that spits out a canned answer to any given button that is pushed. Some dedicated and very successful therapists do not mind sacrificing their own fresh involvement in the spontaneous process of change for the sake of telling a client something he has told a hundred people before. A psychoanalyst explained his rationale for not altering his therapeutic formula: "Look, I've worked a long time to perfect my favorite metaphors. I have no right to exchange them with as yet unproven examples just for my own amusement. Of course I get tired of saying the same things to all my clients; but that's what I'm paid to do."

The other point of view conceives of each therapy session as an individual masterpiece. It may, and probably will, contain elements in common with many other works of art in the same style. The same themes repeat themselves. Basically the process of change follows a predictable pattern, even if the client's individual history and the therapist's characteristic style vary. Such a clinician attempts to translate her energy authentically in every session, to create each therapeutic masterpiece with personalized appeal. In the words of one practitioner: "I have this rule never to repeat myself, or at least not in the precise way I expressed something before. If I don't alter the story, I will tell it in a different way or relate it more specifically to the life of any client. I have this fantasy my clients might someday compare notes about what I told them. I can't stand the idea that they might discover I told them the same thing. Yet, it is much harder on me to stay on my toes, think of new ways to get points across, but it's worth it: I'm always learning and getting better, and I don't get bored."

The practice of therapy can indeed be an exercise in creativity—especially in the ways we play with language. We are playwrights in that we spontaneously compose and direct dialogue, acting out various roles of a nurturer, an authority, or a character from a client's life. We are poets in that we create images and metaphors to illustrate ideas. Over the years most practitioners have hoarded in their heads a wonderful library of helping stories and therapeutic anecdotes they have borrowed or invented. These represent the sum total of a practitioner's life work. One of the things we do so well as we walk through life is to collect things that may be useful in a session at a later time.

Since creativity is essentially the discovery of an analogy on multiple planes that nobody has seen before, therapists are original thinkers of the first order. Take wit and humor as examples. Freud long had an appreciation for humor and a use for wit, and not just as another entry into the unconscious, but as the highest expression of creativity. Therapists use humor and parody to defuse tension with a client, to confront the client in a less threatening way, or to discuss taboo subjects that might be more difficult to approach from a more direct angle. Implicit in a humorous anecdote or pun could be the nucleus of a major insight, one the client may first laugh at before considering the painful truth the punch line contains.

Laughter, we know, has a cathartic value of its own. The therapist's occasional role as a court jester who seeks to coax a smile out of the frozen features of despair represents only one way humor can be used in the therapeutic process. Koestler (1964, pp. 91-92) found humor to be the best single example of how the creative mind works: "To cause surprise the humorist must have a modicum of originality—the ability to break away from the stereotyped routines of thought. Caricaturist, satirist, the writer of nonsense-humour, and even the expert tickler, each operates on more than one plane. Whether his purpose is to convey a social message, or merely to entertain, he must provide mental jolts, caused by the collision of incompatible matrices."

The preceding theory of humor could also be a description of therapy itself—helping people to break away from stereotyped routines, providing mental jolts, and especially encouraging thinking on multiple levels. In this very routine the therapist is a scholar and practitioner of originality par excellence. Each and every client presents us with their perception of a life-threatening crisis or a serious problem that has no solution. Because we are capable of viewing any behavior on many levels, we do not experience the same feelings of being stuck as the client does. We can reframe the problem in a different light, change its shape in such a way that it may more easily be solved. Often, this simple maneuver of looking at the same old problem from a different angle is sufficient in itself to provide immediate relief (Haley, 1973).

Originality is evidenced in the therapist's thinking and behavior in other ways as well. When we stop to consider the conditions likely to spawn creative acts—that is, permissiveness, absence of external criticism, openness to new experience, acceptance of novelty, an emphasis on internal control and individual autonomy, flexible problem solving, integration of cognitive/affective dimensions, psychological safety and support—we realize we are describing the experience of therapy (Rogers, [1954] 1976). Both the client and the therapist interact within an environment that is designed to promote the maximum amount of creative thinking. Each gives the other permission to experiment with new ideas and novel approaches to problem solving. The client is encouraged to consider unusual ways of looking at her life, her goals, and the methods of getting where she wants to be. All the while a client is attempting to go beyond previously defined limits and choices, the therapist is busy processing all the information that has been presented—past history, current functioning, complaints and symptoms, and interaction style are collated in the brain, until finally, there is a startling moment of revelation. By combining all the data in a unique and organized way, a creative interpretation of the client's behavior is invented. Further innovation is required to determine the best way to facilitate the client's insights and, later, to help her act on the knowledge in a constructive manner.

For those therapists who value creativity in their work, innovative strategies become second nature. More importantly, they become less certain of what they already know. For centuries helping professionals were absolutely certain that the mentally afflicted were possessed with demons that needed to be exorcised. It is arrogance of the intellect that has drawn us into the Dark Ages. Those therapists who are possessed with the single-minded devotion to a way of doing things, without consideration for revision and evolution, will hardly advance the state of our profession.

Creative therapists listen to the voice inside them. They pay attention to what does not make sense, even though things may have always been done that way. They are constructive rule breakers. They take cases that make them feel uncomfortable. They treat each case as if it were totally unique. And most of all, they enjoy the company of other people who challenge their ideas. They find their creativity nurtured in the interactions with colleagues and, especially, with clients.

The mutual creative energy fostered in the client and therapist as they encounter one another is a final factor in the chain of consequences that are part of their reciprocal influence. For Bugental (1978) being a therapist is much more than making a buck or belonging to a prestigious profession. It is "an arena for my creativity and endless raw material to feed it. It has been the source of anguish, pain, and anxiety—sometimes in the work itself, but more frequently within myself and with those important in my life in confrontations stimulated directly or indirectly by the impact of the work and relationships with my clients" (pp. 149-150). For Bugental (1976) being a creative therapist involves the process of becoming more aware. It is not necessary for us to do anything to ourselves, to change anything in our lives, to alter our style of helping. Rather, we can be more aware of ourselves just as we are. This process involves recovering our own vision that has become unduly influenced by our mentors and not influenced enough by our own experiences.

Our clients do indeed change us almost as much as we change them. Even though we know and understand the rules and enforce them, guard against infection by clients, even though they are amateurs at influence, befuddled and distracted as they are with their own concerns, we cannot remain completely unaffected. We are touched by their goodness and the joy and privilege we feel in being allowed to get so close to a human soul. And we are harmed by their malicious and destructive energy. Whenever we enter a room with another life in great torment, we will find no escape from our own despair. And we will find no way to hold down the elation we feel as a witness to another person's transformation—just as we are the catalyst for our own.

References

Alexander, F. G., and Selesnick, S. T. *The History of Psychiatry*. New York: Mentor, 1966.

Anthony, C. P., and Thibodeau, G. A. *Textbook of Anatomy and Physiology*. St. Louis, Mo.: Mosby, 1979.

Bach, G. "The George Bach Self-Recognition Inventory for Burned-Out Therapists." *Voices*, 1979, *15* (2), 73-77.

Bandler, R., and Grinder, J. *Frogs into Princes*. Moab, Utah: Real People Press, 1979.

Bandura, A. *Social Learning Theory*. Englewood Cliffs, N.J.: Prentice-Hall, 1977.

Bellack, L., and Faithorn, P. *Crises and Special Problems in Psychoanalysis and Psychotherapy*. New York: Brunner/Mazel, 1981.

Bloom, M. *The Paradox of Helping*. New York: Wiley, 1975.

Boorstein, D. *The Discoverers*. New York: Random House, 1983.

Boy, A. V., and Pine, G. J. *Client-Centered Counseling: A Renewal*. Newton, Mass.: Allyn & Bacon, 1982.

Breuer, G. *Sociobiology and the Human Dimension*. Cambridge, England: Cambridge University Press, 1982.

Bronowski, J. *The Origins of Knowledge and Imagination*. New Haven, Conn.: Yale University Press, 1978.

Bugental, J. F. T. *The Search for Existential Identity: Patient-*

Therapist Dialogues in Humanistic Psychotherapy. San Francisco: Jossey-Bass, 1976.

Bugental, J. F. T. *Psychotherapy and Process.* Reading, Mass.: Addison-Wesley, 1978.

Burton, A. "Healing as a Lifestyle." In A. Burton and Associates (eds.), *Twelve Therapists: How They Live and Actualize Themselves.* San Francisco: Jossey-Bass, 1972.

Campbell, K. "The Psychotherapy Relationship with Borderline Personality Disorders." *Psychotherapy: Theory, Research, and Practice,* 1982, *19* (2), 166–193.

Carroll, L. *Through the Looking-Glass.* New York: Bantam, 1981. (Originally published 1871.)

Castaneda, C. *A Separate Reality.* New York: Simon & Schuster, 1971.

Caughey, J. L. "Media Mentors." *Psychology Today,* Sept. 1978, pp. 44–49.

Cerney, M. S. "Countertransference Revisited." *Journal of Counseling and Development,* 1985, *63,* 362–364.

Chessick, R. "The Sad Soul of the Psychiatrist." *Bulletin of the Menninger Clinic,* 1978, *42* (1), 1–10.

Combs, A. V., Avila, D. L., and Purkey, W. W. *Helping Relationships.* Newton, Mass.: Allyn & Bacon, 1971.

Corey, G. *Theory and Practice of Counseling and Psychotherapy.* (3rd ed.) Monterey, Calif.: Brooks/Cole, 1986.

Csikszentmihalyi, M. *Beyond Boredom and Anxiety: The Experience of Play in Work and Games.* San Francisco: Jossey-Bass, 1975.

Curtis, J. M. "The Effect of Therapist Self-Disclosure on Patients' Perceptions of Empathy, Competence, and Trust in an Analogue Psychotherapeutic Interaction." *Psychotherapy: Theory, Research, and Practice,* 1982, *19* (1), 54–62.

Dai, B. "My Experience of Psychotherapy." *Voices,* 1979, *15* (2), 26–33.

Donleavy, J. P. *The Unexpurgated Code.* New York: Delta, 1975.

Dorn, F. J. "The Social Influence Model: A Social Psychological Approach to Counseling." *Personnel and Guidance Journal,* Feb. 1984, pp. 342–345.

Dyer, W. W., and Vriend, J. *Counseling Techniques that Work.* New York: Funk & Wagnalls, 1977.

Edelwich, J., and Brodsky, A. *Burn-Out.* New York: Human Sciences Press, 1980.

Ellis, A. "Psychotherapy Without Tears." In A. Burton and Associates (eds.), *Twelve Therapists: How They Live and Actualize Themselves.* San Francisco: Jossey-Bass, 1972.

Ellis, A. Article. *Psychotherapy in Private Practice,* 1983, *1* (1).

Ellis, A. "How to Deal with Your Most Difficult Client—You." *Psychotherapy in Private Practice,* 1984, *2* (1), 25–34.

English, O. S. "How I Found My Way to Psychiatry." In A. Burton and Associates (eds.), *Twelve Therapists: How They Live and Actualize Themselves.* San Francisco: Jossey-Bass, 1972.

Erickson, M. "An Hypnotic Technique for Resistant Patients." *American Journal of Clinical Hypnosis,* 1964, *1,* 8–32.

Erikson, E. *Childhood and Society.* New York: Norton, 1963.

Farber, B. A. "The Effects of Psychotherapeutic Practice upon Psychotherapists." *Psychotherapy: Theory, Research, and Practice,* 1983, *20* (2), 174–182.

Fine, H. J. "Despair and Depletion in the Therapist." *Psychotherapy: Theory, Research, and Practice,* 1980, *17* (4), 392–395.

Fine, R. "Search for Love." In A. Burton and Associates (eds.), *Twelve Therapists: How They Live and Actualize Themselves.* San Francisco: Jossey-Bass, 1972.

Fisch, R., Weakland, J. H., and Segal, L. *The Tactics of Change: Doing Therapy Briefly.* San Francisco: Jossey-Bass, 1982.

Fish, J. M. *Placebo Therapy: A Practical Guide to Social Influence in Psychotherapy.* San Francisco: Jossey-Bass, 1973.

Fisher, K. "Charges Catch Clinicians in Cycle of Shame, Slip Ups." *APA Monitor,* 1985, *16* (5), 6–7.

Fitzgerald, F. S. *Tender Is the Night.* New York: Scribner's, 1933.

Frank, J. D. *Persuasion and Healing.* New York: Schocken, 1961.

Frank, R. "Money and Other Trade-Offs in Psychotherapy." *Voices,* 1979, *14* (4), 42–44.

Freud, A. "The Widening Scope of Indication for Psychoanalysis." *Journal of American Psychoanalytic Association,* 1954, *2,* 607–620.

Freud, S. "The Dynamics of Transference." In *Collected Papers.* Vol. 8. London: Imago, 1912.

Freud, S. "Analysis: Terminable or Interminable." In *Collected Papers.* Vol. 5. London: Hogarth Press, 1950. (Originally published 1937.)

Freud, S. *The Origins of Psychoanalysis.* New York: Basic Books, 1954. (Originally published 1897.)

Freud, S. "Letter to Ferenczi, Oct. 6, 1910." In E. Jones, *The Life and Work of Sigmund Freud.* Vol. 2. New York: Basic Books, 1955.

Freudenberger, H. J. "The Staff Burn-Out Syndrome in Alternative Institutions." *Psychotherapy: Theory, Research, and Practice,* 1975, *12* (1), 73–82.

Gordon, D. *Therapeutic Metaphors.* Cupertino, Calif.: Meta Publications, 1978.

Griswell, G. E. "Dead Tired and Bone Weary." *Voices,* 1979, *152,* 49–53.

Gross, D., and Kahn, J. "Values of Three Practitioner Groups." *Journal of Counseling and Values,* 1983, *28* (1), 228–333.

Haley, J. *Ordeal Therapy: Unusual Ways to Change Behavior.* San Francisco: Jossey-Bass, 1984.

Haley, J. *Uncommon Therapy.* New York: Norton, 1973.

Harrison, J. *Sundog.* New York: Dutton, 1984.

Hayward, J. W. *Perceiving Ordinary Magic.* Boulder, Colo.: New Science Library, 1984.

Healy, S. D. *Boredom, Self, and Culture.* Madison, N.J.: Fairleigh Dickinson University Press, 1984.

Henry, W. E. "Some Observations on the Lives of Healers." *Human Development,* 1966, *9,* 47–56.

Henry, W. E., Sims, J. H., and Spray, S. L. *Public and Private Lives of Psychotherapists.* San Francisco: Jossey-Bass, 1973.

Herron, W. G., and Rouslin, S. *Issues in Psychotherapy.* Washington, D.C.: Oryn Publications, 1984.

Holroyd, J. C., and Brodsky, A. M. "Psychologists' Attitudes and Practices Regarding Erotic and Nonerotic Physical Contact with Patients." *American Psychologist*, 1977, *32*, 843-849.

Jourard, S. M. *The Transparent Self.* New York: D. Van Nostrand, 1971.

Kagan, N. "Can Technology Help Us Toward Reliability in Influencing Human Interaction." In J. Vriend and W. W. Dyer (eds.), *Counseling Effectively in Groups.* Englewood Cliffs, N.J.: Educational Technology, 1973.

Keen, S. "Boredom and How to Beat It." *Psychology Today*, May 1977, pp. 78-84.

Kennedy, W. *Ironweed.* New York: Viking, 1983.

Keyes, R. *Chancing It: Why We Take Risks.* Boston: Little, Brown, 1985.

Kierkegaard, S. *Either/Or.* Princeton, N.J.: Princeton University Press, 1944.

Klopfer, W. G. "The Seductive Patient." In W. G. Klopfer and M. R. Reed (eds.), *Problems in Psychotherapy.* New York: Wiley, 1974.

Koestler, A. *The Act of Creation.* New York: Dell, 1964.

Kopp, S. *If You Meet the Buddah on the Road, Kill Him!* Palo Alto, Calif.: Science and Behavior Books, 1972.

Kopp, S. *Even a Stone Can Be a Teacher.* Los Angeles: Tarcher, 1985.

Kottler, J. A. *Pragmatic Group Leadership.* Monterey, Calif.: Brooks/Cole, 1983.

Kovacs, A. L. "The Emotional Hazards of Teaching Psychotherapy." *Psychotherapy: Theory, Research, and Practice*, 1976, *13* (4), 321-334.

Kramer, R., and Weiner, I. "Psychiatry on the Borderline." *Psychotherapy Today*, Nov. 1983, pp. 70-73.

Lamb, F. B. *Wizard of the Upper Amazon.* Boston: Houghton Mifflin, 1971.

Levinson, D. *The Seasons of a Man's Life.* New York: Knopf, 1978.

London, P. *The Modes and Morals of Psychotherapy.* (2nd ed.) New York: Hemisphere, 1985.

Lowen, A. *Narcissism.* New York: Macmillan, 1983.

Madanes, C. *Strategic Family Therapy.* San Francisco: Jossey-Bass, 1981.

Martin, E. S., and Schurtman, R. "Termination Anxiety as It Affects the Therapist." *Psychotherapy: Theory, Research, and Practice,* 1985, *22* (1), 92–96.

Maslach, C. *Burnout: The Cost of Caring.* Englewood Cliffs, N.J.: Prentice-Hall, 1982.

Maslow, A. *Toward a Psychology of Being.* New York: D. Van Nostrand, 1968.

Masterson, J. F. *Countertransference and Psychotherapeutic Technique.* New York: Brunner/Mazel, 1983.

May, R. *Existence.* New York: Simon & Schuster, 1958.

May, R. *The Courage to Create.* New York: Norton, 1975.

May, R. *The Discovery of Being.* New York: Norton, 1983.

May, R. "Rollo May: The Case for Love, Beauty and the Humanities" (interview by S. Cunningham). *APA Monitor,* May 1985, p. 17.

Minuchin, S., and Fishman, H. C. *Family Therapy Techniques.* Cambridge, Mass.: Harvard University Press, 1981.

Morgan, W. P. "The Mind of the Marathoner." *Psychology Today,* Apr. 1978, pp. 38–47.

Moss, R. *The I That Is We.* Berkeley, Calif.: Celestial Arts, 1981.

Napier, A. Y., and Whitaker, C. A. *The Family Crucible.* New York: Bantam Books, 1978.

Nash, J., Norcross, J. C., and Prochaska, J. O. "Satisfaction and Stresses of Independent Practice." *Psychotherapy in Private Practice,* 1984, *2* (4), 39–48.

Palmer, J. O. *A Primer of Eclectic Psychotherapy.* Monterey, Calif.: Brooks/Cole, 1980.

Patterson, C. H. "What Is the Placebo in Psychotherapy?" *Psychotherapy: Theory, Research, and Practice,* 1985, *22* (2), 163–169.

Peck, M. S. *The Road Less Traveled.* New York: Simon & Schuster, 1978.

Penzer, W. N. "The Psychopathology of the Psychotherapist." *Psychotherapy in Private Practice,* 1984, *2* (2), 51–59.

Perry, M. A., and Furukawa, J. M. "Modeling Methods." In F. H. Kanfer and A. P. Goldstein (eds.), *Helping People Change*. New York: Pergamon, 1980.

Pines, A. M., Aronson, E., and Kafry, D. *Burnout*. New York: Free Press, 1981.

Polster, E. "Stolen by Gypsies." In A. Burton and Associates (eds.), *Twelve Therapists: How They Live and Actualize Themselves*. San Francisco: Jossey-Bass, 1972.

Pope, K. S., Keith-Spiegel, P., and Tabachnick, B. G. "Sexual Attraction to Clients." *American Psychologist*, 1986, *41* (2), 147-156.

Rainer, T. *The New Diary*. Los Angeles: Tarcher, 1978.

Ram Dass and Gorman, P. *How Can I Help? Stories and Reflections on Service*. New York: Knopf, 1985.

Robbins, T. *Still Life of Woodpecker*. New York: Bantam Books, 1980.

Rogers, C. "My Personal Growth." In A. Burton and Associates (eds.), *Twelve Therapists: How They Live and Actualize Themselves*. San Francisco: Jossey-Bass, 1972.

Rogers, C. R. "Toward a Theory of Creativity." In A. Rothenberg and C. R. Hausman (eds.), *The Creativity Question*. Durham, N.C.: Duke University Press, 1978. (Originally published 1954.)

de Saint-Exupéry, A. *The Little Prince*. New York: Harcourt Brace Jovanovich, 1943.

Satir, V., and Baldwin, M. *Satir Step by Step*. Palo Alto, Calif.: Science and Behavior Books, 1983.

Schneiderman, S. *Jacques Lacan: The Death of an Intellectual Hero*. Cambridge, Mass.: Harvard University Press, 1983.

Schön, D. A. *The Reflective Practitioner*. New York: Basic Books, 1983.

Shepard, M. *A Psychiatrist's Head*. New York: Dell, 1972.

Silverstein, S. *The Giving Tree*. New York: Harper & Row, 1964.

Sinclair, J. D. "How the Mind Recharges Batteries." *Psychology Today*, Nov. 1982, p. 96.

Smith, A. "The Benefits of Boredom." *Psychology Today*, Apr. 1976, pp. 46-51.

Spense, D. P. *Narrative and Historical Truth.* New York: Norton, 1982.

Stein, H. *Ethics and Other Liabilities.* New York: St. Martin's Press, 1982.

Steinzor, B. "Mystery of Self and Other." In A. Burton and Associates (eds.), *Twelve Therapists: How They Live and Actualize Themselves.* San Francisco: Jossey-Bass, 1972.

Strong, S. "Emerging Integrations of Clinical and Social Psychology: A Clinician's Perspective." In G. Weary and H. Mirels (eds.), *Integrations of Clinical and Social Psychology.* New York: Oxford University Press, 1982.

Strupp, H. H. "Humanism and Psychotherapy: A Personal Statement of the Therapist's Essential Values." *Psychotherapy: Theory, Research, and Practice,* 1980, *17* (4), 396–400.

Thomas, L. *The Medusa and the Snail.* New York: Viking Penguin, 1974.

Van Hoose, W. H., and Kottler, J. A. *Ethical and Legal Issues in Counseling and Psychotherapy.* (2nd ed.) San Francisco: Jossey-Bass, 1985.

Viscott, D. *Risking.* New York: Pocket Books, 1977.

Vriend, J., and Dyer, W. W. *Counseling for Personal Mastery* (A tape series). Washington, D.C.: Association for Counseling and Development Press, 1973.

Warkentin, J. "Paradox of Being Alien and Intimate." In A. Burton and Associates (eds.), *Twelve Therapists: How They Live and Actualize Themselves.* San Francisco: Jossey-Bass, 1972.

Watkins, C. E. "Countertransference: Its Impact on the Counseling Situation." *Journal of Counseling and Development,* 1985, *63,* 356–359.

Weil, A. *Health and Healing.* Boston: Houghton Mifflin, 1983.

Weiner, M. F. *The Psychotherapeutic Impasse.* New York: Free Press, 1982.

Weisman, A. "Confrontation, Countertransference, and Context." In G. Adler and P. G. Myerson (eds.), *Confrontation in Psychotherapy.* New York: Science House, 1973.

Wicker, A. W. "Getting Out of Conceptual Ruts." *American Psychologist,* Oct. 1985, pp. 1094–1103.

Wilber, K. *Eye to Eye.* Garden City, N.Y.: Anchor Books, 1983.

Wolfe, T. *The Notebooks of Thomas Wolfe,* R. S. Kennedy and P. Reeves (eds.). Chapel Hill: University of North Carolina Press, 1970. (Originally published 1921.)

Yalom, I. D. *Existential Psychotherapy.* New York: Basic Books, 1980.

Zelen, S. L. "Sexualization of Therapeutic Relationships: The Dual Vulnerability of Patient and Therapist." *Psychotherapy: Theory, Research, and Practice,* 1985, *22* (2), 178-185.

Index